Community Profiling

Second edition

nch
2/12/08

Community Profiling

A practical guide

Second edition

Murray Hawtin and Janie Percy-Smith

Open University Press

Open University Press
McGraw-Hill Education
McGraw-Hill House
Shoppenhangers Road
Maidenhead
Berkshire
England
SL6 2QL

email: enquiries@openup.co.uk
world wide web: www.openup.co.uk

and Two Penn Plaza, New York, NY 10121-2289, USA

First edition published 1994
Reprinted 1994, 1995 (twice), 1996, 1998
This second edition published 2007

A catalogue record of this book is available from the British Library

ISBN-13 978-0-33-522164-6 (pb) 978-0-33-522165-3 (hb)
ISBN-10 0-33-522164-5 (pb) 0-33-522165-3 (hb)

Library of Congress Cataloging-in-Publication Data
CIP data applied for

Typeset by RefineCatch Limited, Bungay, Suffolk
Printed in Poland EU by OzGraf S.A
www.polskabook.pl

The *McGraw·Hill* Companies

Contents

List of figures

Preface to second edition

It has been over 12 years since we produced the first edition of *Community Profiling: Auditing Social Needs*. At the time we did not imagine what a success the book would be, nor how useful it would prove to be for students and practitioners in so many fields. The idea for the book initially grew out of a short pamphlet entitled *Finding Out About Your Community: How To Do a Social Audit* published by the then Policy Research Unit, Leeds Metropolitan University, in 1990. This early publication was intended as a guide for community groups and community practitioners wanting to undertake their own social audits or community profiles. Building on the success of the approach described in the pamphlet, the authors, together with other colleagues in the Policy Research Institute, undertook other social audits and community profiles adding to our experience, understanding and knowledge.

The first edition of this book drew upon the original pamphlet, the experiences gained in the field and discussions with others working on similar community profiling and social auditing projects across the country. Since then, however, the world has moved on in significant ways. The political context of communities has changed since the early 1990s, with the government now more concerned about democratic renewal and the role of local authorities as community leaders and taking an active role in 'place shaping'. But most striking of all, the technologies around accessing information have developed almost beyond recognition since we first wrote the book. Any community group with access to a computer and the internet can now find masses of information about their locality without even setting foot outside.

To reflect these changes we have had to substantially rewrite several of the chapters in this new edition of the book. However, the essence of the book remains the same. It is still intended to serve as a practical guide for anyone who is engaged in community profiling, social auditing, needs assessment or community consultation, especially community workers and community practitioners across a range of disciplines including regeneration, neighbourhood management, library services, housing, health, youth work and social care. We hope that it will also continue to be a useful resource for voluntary and community organizations as well as social science and other students who are required to undertake community-based research.

We have maintained an important principle from the first edition, which is that the book works on a 'need-to-know' basis. It is not a comprehensive review of social science research methods; there are many other texts which serve this function, some of which we reference. Rather, we provide a basic, step-by-step guide for those wishing to undertake a community profile or social audit with as much technical information as is necessary to do a good enough job. The guide is aimed particularly at those with a basic or limited knowledge of research methods and techniques and probably only limited resources. We have therefore kept the detailed description of the methods to a minimum in the main text, but have added an appendix (Appendix 2) that gives sufficient detail for those who wish to carry out more complex research. Also, for those interested in following up particular aspects in more detail, the guides to further reading and resources which appear in Appendix 3 should be of help. The glossary (Appendix 1) is a new addition and we hope that the definitions of some of the more technical terms used throughout the book will be of help to readers.

This book is a distillation of the knowledge, skills, expertise and experience not only of the authors but also of a much wider group of people. Although the book is the sole responsibility of the current authors, we recognize with gratitude and appreciation the contributions of our colleagues past and present at the Policy Research Institute and those of others elsewhere with whom we have discussed ideas over many years. In addition, we acknowledge with thanks the contributions of all those communities who have allowed us to profile them, assess their needs or do social auditing work in their midst. We hope that this practical research experience in and with communities is reflected in the style, tone and approach of this book.

1 What is a community profile?

At the time of publication of the first edition of this book **community profiling** was regarded very much as a tool for community development. This is still the case. However, in addition there has been an increasing emphasis by policy makers and practitioners on community profiling as a useful foundation for a wide range of policy and service delivery-related processes.

In this first chapter we briefly review the development of community profiling as an approach before discussing the similarities and differences between community profiling and other related types of community-based research. A definition of community profiling is then proposed and discussed and the remainder of the book then sketched out.

Development of community profiling

Community profiling as a tool of **community development** is not new (see Baldock 1974; Milson 1974; Henderson and Thomas 1987). Many people will remember the community self-surveys that were undertaken in the 1970s; others will be aware of similar work undertaken in the USA and the Netherlands as early as the 1950s. During the 1980s and 1990s, a group of related techniques – community profiling, **needs assessments**, **social audits** and **community consultations** – enjoyed a new lease of life. In particular the 1980s saw the widespread use of the term 'social audit' to describe studies that sought to demonstrate the impact on communities of changes in public policy or of major factory closures (see, for example, Merseyside County Council 1983; Newcastle City Council 1985). At about the same time, the Archbishop of Canterbury's Report, *Faith in the City* (1985), was published, which suggested that inner-city churches might undertake parish audits as a means of reassessing their role in urban communities.

The 1990s saw a series of central government initiatives aimed at local areas which required assessments of local needs or community consultations to be carried out. These included Community Care, City Challenge, Neighbourhood Renewal and Estate Action. These trends continued through the 1990s and into the 2000s with the Single Regeneration Budget, New Deal for Communities, Neighbourhood Renewal Funding, Neighbourhood Management and the requirement on local authorities to produce Community Strategies. (Current and recent policy drivers for community profiles are discussed in more detail in Chapter 2.)

At the same time many local authorities have harnessed new technology to produce statistical profiles and maps that identify areas with particular problems – high levels of crime, educational under-achievement, poverty or disadvantage – as a means of targeting resources more effectively. In addition some authorities have used, and continue to use, community profiles as an element in the development of strategies to devolve decision making and service delivery down to neighbourhood level. Others have recognized their use in developing baselines which can then be used in the monitoring, review and evaluation of policies and programmes. Most recently the Audit Commission has encouraged local authorities to construct **area profiles** which, it argues, 'place strong emphasis on people and place and on issues that cut across service boundaries, for example a picture of the needs of specific sectors of the community, such as older citizens' (Audit Commission 2006).

Increasingly, too, a wide range of statutory agencies have been interested in obtaining feedback from their 'customers', reflecting a changing emphasis on the needs of the customer as opposed to those of the service provider.

Communities, community groups and voluntary organizations have also initiated or conducted community profiling exercises as a means of demonstrating to statutory service providers that they are not receiving an adequate level of services, or that they have needs that are not currently being met, or to demonstrate opposition to initiatives that will adversely affect them. And, finally, community development workers and other patch-based front-line providers continue to use profiling exercises of various kinds as a means of 'getting to know their patch', and also to help build confidence and capacity within local communities. (These different uses of community profiling are discussed further in Chapter 2.)

Needs assessment, community consultation, social audit or community profile

Needs assessment, community consultation, social audit and community profile are all terms that can be found in the literature and in practice to refer to exercises that appear to share some common features. However, while there are some similarities between them there are also some important differences.

The answers to the following questions provide an indication of points of convergence or divergence.

- What is the purpose of the exercise?
- Who is initiating it?
- To what extent is the community involved?
- What is the scope of the exercise and who has determined this?

Needs assessment

In general, needs assessments tend to be initiated and/or carried out by a statutory agency, for example a Primary Care Trust (PCT) or local authority department, for policy planning purposes (Percy-Smith 1996: 1–9). Needs assessments generally make use of existing data (for example, population data), although this may be supplemented with additional sources that provide intelligence on attitudes to, and perceptions of, local needs on the part of those most likely to be affected by a service. An example of the needs assessment approach are the housing needs assessments that have to be carried out in most local areas. More recently local authorities have been required to undertake assessments of the needs of children living in the local area as part of the move towards the development of Children's Trust arrangements.

Communities are not always involved in the needs assessment process. Sometimes this is because the geographical or administrative area to be covered is too large for communities to be involved in any practical sense. Or it may be because the resources available for the needs assessment – including financial resources, time and expertise – are in short supply in the agencies concerned. Nevertheless, while needs assessments undertaken at the level of the wider administrative area may not include many opportunities for **primary research** (collecting new information) or **community involvement**, there have been a number of more local needs assessments undertaken by community practitioners wanting to develop services more attuned to the needs of people on their 'patch'. And, indeed, the whole area of **practitioner research** is increasing in part as a result of the requirement that practice is evidence-based (see Chapter 2).

Community consultations

Increasingly public bodies across a wide spectrum of policy areas are obliged, or are strongly advised, to carry out consultations with their local community. Such consultations have, in recent years, become increasingly sophisticated, making use of a variety of different techniques that go beyond the standard **survey** questionnaire to include: **focus groups**, online questionnaires, **citizens' panels** and **citizens' juries**, and **Planning for Real** exercises. Although many of these exercises have been criticized as being, in practice, perfunctory and not intended to bring about real change in the policies or programmes of the agencies carrying them out, there are, nonetheless, many examples of consultations that do constitute genuine attempts to seek out the views of local people.

Community consultations, unlike community profiles, social audits or needs assessments, typically take place in relation to a set of proposals, options or priorities that have already been developed by the initiating agency or to assess satisfaction with an existing service. They could, however, be used as one element in a broader community profiling, social auditing or needs assessment exercise.

Social audit

The term social audit has come to refer to a specific process that has been advocated and carried out by, in particular, the New Economics Foundation (2006). Social auditing (or **social accounting** as it is sometimes known) is a way of measuring and reporting on an organization's performance that takes account of social and ethical impacts. Just as a financial audit can reveal the financial health of an organization through an examination of its accounts, so, it is argued, a social audit can reveal the 'health' of a company or enterprise. And this approach can also be applied to an examination of the health of a community which results from the interplay of public services, housing, employment, the natural and social environment and many other factors.

Social audits may be conducted at a community level and involve the collection of new primary data about the perceptions of those living or working in that community, or at the city or district level where the focus tends to be more on identifying inequities between communities for the purpose of reallocating resources. In such cases, the information used to compile the audit is more likely to be data that is already in existence, for example health statistics, housing benefit data, unemployment data and information on service provision derived from service departments themselves.

Community profile

The term 'community profile' is the broadest of those under discussion in that it is typically used to refer to a range of projects undertaken or initiated by different organizations including communities themselves, statutory agencies and **voluntary organizations**. Community profiles are also potentially broadest in scope, covering both needs and resources and the whole range of issues affecting communities. What is perhaps distinctive about community profiles is the extent to which the community is involved. Whereas needs assessments and social audits may benefit from the active involvement of the community, in practice this does not always occur. However, a good community profile, in our view, does require active community involvement.

Because 'community profile' is the term which has the broadest application and because it is most likely to conform to certain principles of community development described in the next section, this is the term that we will generally use throughout this book, except where approaches or techniques are discussed that relate particularly to needs assessment, community consultation or social audit.

A community profile might, then, be defined as follows:

> A *comprehensive* description of the *needs* of a population that is defined, or defines itself, as a *community*, and the *resources* that exist within that community, carried out with the *active involvement of the community* itself, for the purpose of developing an *action plan* or other means of improving the quality of life of the community.

The component parts of this definition are justified and explained further in the next section.

Elements of a community profile

Our proposed definition suggests that a community profile should be *comprehensive* in coverage. We are not suggesting that all community profiles are, in practice, comprehensive; rather that in planning a community profile consideration needs to be given to how different aspects of the life of the community are interrelated. The totality of individuals' and communities' lives do not conform to departmental, agency, service or policy boundaries. The issues which people experience in their everyday lives cannot, typically, be defined as 'housing problems' or 'health' or 'social isolation'. Rather, issues often interact in such a way that the whole is greater than the sum of the constituent parts. Of course, social researchers and those charged with meeting needs and providing services know about the relationship between, for example, poor housing and ill health or unemployment and depression. However, practice has often been slow to reflect this reality. So policies designed to combat poor housing, ill health, unemployment and mental health problems are still, often, formulated and implemented in isolation from each other. Community profiles that are comprehensive in their coverage will help challenge bureaucratic departmentalism as well as more accurately reflecting the reality of people's lives. Christakopoulou *et al.* (2001) suggest that a comprehensive community profile ought to address the following aspects of people's lives:

- *the area as a place to live* – including the quality of the physical environment and people's attitudes to living there; the extent to which needs are matched with resources; and the extent to which local facilities meet people's goals and aspirations;
- *the area as a social community* – including residents' involvement in the social life of the community; the extent to which the community is supportive; formal and informal networks;
- *the area as an economic community* – including income levels and employment prospects of local residents; prosperity and viability of local shops;
- *the area as a political community* – including systems and structures of political representation and local area management; the extent to which local people can influence decisions that affect them; the degree of involvement in local decision making; participation in **community organizations**;
- *the area as a personal space* – the degree of attachment that people have to the local area; memories and life experiences of local people;
- *the area as part of its city* – infrastructural, economic and social linkages between the local area and the city or district of which it is a part; the specific local identity that differentiates the community from the rest of the area/district.

Our definition refers to *needs* and *resources*, both of which are important for a full understanding of a community. By resources we mean assets held in the area and put to use for the benefit of the community. These might include, for example, the housing stock, parks, hospitals and clinics, community centres, places of worship and schools as well as people's time and expertise made available to others, or the employment opportunities within a given area and their product, service or wealth-distributing function. In any community there are also under-utilized resources; it may be important to find out why they are under-utilized and how they might be utilized more effectively. There are also likely to be potential resources, for example derelict buildings or vacant land which, while they serve no useful purpose at the moment, could be put to the use of the community if they were appropriately developed.

When we talk about resources we also mean those intangible resources that are a source of strength and potential within the community. These might include such things as the skills – both formal and informal – of members of the community; networks of informal support such as families, households and neighbours; more formal support such as self-help and community organizations; and qualities and characteristics that exist within the community such as resilience, determination, trust, community-mindedness and the extent of volunteering or active citizenship. Many of these characteristics have come to be summed up by the term '**social capital**'. It is important to document the existence of social capital since to focus solely on what is needy about a community can not only be disheartening, perhaps reinforcing a negative image which community members are trying to change, but is also likely to be only a partial picture.

Resources are often seen simply in terms of money and this is, of course, an important resource for any community. Social audits have, in particular, been used to show how much money is deployed in the running of services in an area and to reveal whether there is a just distribution of public resources in terms of the needs of particular communities (see, for example, London Borough of Southwark 1987). The injection of extra money is often seen to be the only way of addressing unmet needs; however, this may not always be the most appropriate or effective approach. There might be different ways of using existing resources or delivering existing services. The neighbourhood management approach is aiming to achieve this by bringing the management of local services closer to the neighbourhood level and, in doing so, 'bending' mainstream provision to meet local needs better. A social audit could point to new ways of employing local people in the delivery of local services and retaining resources within the area.

The concept of *need* features prominently in community profiles. Although it is a contested concept (Doyal and Gough 1991), there is, nonetheless, an acceptance that need is a legitimate basis on which to make at least some decisions about the allocation of resources. As such it is an important component of a community profile. However, community profiles differ from needs assessments because of their focus on resources as well as needs, their emphasis on a participative approach and their action orientation.

In Chapter 3 we discuss at some length some of the different meanings attached to the term community. In this introductory chapter we simply draw attention to some of the different ways of thinking about community. Perhaps the most common idea is that of a group of people who live or work in the same geographical location, for example a housing estate, village or neighbourhood. For some purposes we might want to define a community in terms of an administrative area such as a school catchment area, social services area or PCT area; however, in most cases these areas would be too large to permit active community involvement in a community profiling exercise.

A different way of thinking about a community is in terms of a group of people with a shared or common interest or set of characteristics. For example, people working in the same industry might be assumed for certain purposes to share common interests even though they do not live in the same geographical area. Similarly, women, a minority ethnic group, children or people with disabilities might all be considered as communities of interest for certain purposes. However, it should be noted that this approach can be problematic since it may assign to a particular group a communality of interest that does not, in reality, exist. For example, minority ethnic communities may share some interests and experiences but nonetheless be deeply divided along lines of gender or generation. This may not invalidate the notion of a minority ethnic 'community' but should simply alert us to the possibility or even likelihood of 'communities within communities'. This is, of course, also true of geographically located communities. The diversity and divisions that exist within all communities have important implications for the kinds of community profiling methods that are used (see Chapters 5 and 7).

Our definition of a community profile includes the notion of *active community involvement*. While it is possible to profile a community without the active involvement of local people, we would argue that important information and insights will be lost if this is the case. A profile that is undertaken with the full cooperation and involvement of the community is likely to result in a fuller, more comprehensive and accurate description of that community and, as such, form a better basis on which to build an action plan. Involvement in producing a community profile can also be one way in which a community can become empowered through the development of skills, confidence and awareness of issues (Skinner 1997). Active involvement in the production of a community profile can, therefore, be an important part of a wider process of community development (see also Packham 1998). Chapter 3 includes a discussion of ways of encouraging active involvement of the community including harder to reach groups.

The final part of our definition refers to the idea of the community profile leading to the development of an *action plan* or other means of improving the quality of life of the community. The emphasis, here, is on the importance of community profiling exercises being purposeful and action-oriented (see also Twelvetrees 1991). Producing a description of a community at one point in time will simply add to the archives of the local history group and will achieve very little except a sense of cynicism that time, energy and enthusiasm have been expended for no reason. The aim of the community profile must be to act as a catalyst for the improvement of the quality of life of members of that community. Moving from the identification of needs and resources through the community profiling process to the production of a local action plan which identifies issues, priorities and actions to be taken, sets goals and targets and proposes a means of monitoring their achievement is an important next step.

An important early task in the community profiling process is determining who the audience for the finished product is likely to be. This, in turn, will influence how the final profile is produced: a written report, a glossy pamphlet, an exhibition, a DVD, CD-Rom or some other means of conveying the information. The key to effective communication is to ensure that the methods and approach used are appropriate to the audience and the kinds of impact that are being sought. We examine this issue in greater detail in Chapter 9.

As important as the constituent elements of our definition of a community profile are the values that underpin the approach. The best community profiles are those which not only efficiently and accurately collect, analyse and present information, but which do so in a way that reflects adherence to, and practical implementation of, a set of values. The first of these is respect for the community being profiled. The practical impact of this is that, as far as possible, members of the community are involved in the profiling process in such a way that they gain something positive from the experience beyond the information being collected and that they do not feel that the profile is something that is being 'done to them'. The benefits could include greater confidence in themselves as a community, the building of skills and capacities and a better sense of their own potential. It also means that members of the community must be listened to and their views incorporated at an early stage in the profiling process so that the design of the project reflects their concerns. At the fieldwork stage the implication is that information is collected with sensitivity and confidentiality is respected. It also means that the process adheres to the basic principles of equality by not giving undue weight to any particular views and, conversely, does not exclude or undervalue the views of certain groups.

Structure of the book

The rest of this book is intended to take the reader through the various stages in the community profiling process, beginning with a chapter entitled 'Why do a community profile?', which puts community profiling into the current policy context and examines the relevance of community profiling to that context. Chapter 3 takes readers through the important process of planning a community profile. Chapter 4 examines the range of stakeholders who might be involved in aspects of the community profiling process and ways of involving them. Chapter 5 helps the reader select the methods best suited to the kind of profile they want to produce, and Chapters 6 and 7 discuss particular methods in more detail. Chapter 8 provides advice on how to analyse data in order to turn it into useful information. Chapter 9 examines the issue of what to do with the profile once it has been completed, and ways of maximizing its impact. Finally, Chapter 10 will draw together the key issues raised throughout the book.

At the end of each chapter a list of references can be found. In addition, at the end of the book, you can find an annotated list of further reading and resources. A glossary of key terms used throughout the book can be found in an appendix; where a word or phrase that appears in the glossary is mentioned for the first time it appears in bold in the text. In addition there is also an appendix which provides further detail on some of the more technical aspects of the research methods referred to in the text.

Summary of key issues

Needs assessments, social audits, community consultations and community profiles all share some common characteristics in that they involve obtaining information from and about communities. However, they can also be distinguished from each other in terms of the agencies that are typically involved, the scope and purpose of the exercise and the extent of community involvement.

Community profiling is the broadest of these terms and is the main focus of this book. A community profile can be defined as:

> A comprehensive description of the needs of a population that is defined, or defines itself, as a community, and the resources that exist within that community, carried out with the active involvement of the community itself, for the purpose of developing an action plan or other means of improving the quality of life of the community.

The key words in this definition are: comprehensive, needs, resources, community, active involvement and action plan.

Community profiles are undertaken by a range of different agencies for different purposes. For example, statutory agencies may be required by central government to assess local needs; they may use community profiles as a means of obtaining accurate information of relevance to policy planning, implementation, monitoring and evaluation. Alternatively voluntary or community organizations may initiate a community profile as a means of demonstrating the existence of unmet needs or inadequate resources, or as a part of a community campaign. They may also use community profiles as a means of providing baseline information to be used as a benchmark for assessing future development. Community profiles, if they conform to certain important criteria, can also be used as part of a broader community development strategy.

References

Archbishop of Canterbury's Commission on Urban Priority Areas (1985) *Faith in the City: A Call for Action by Church and Nation*. London: Church House.
Audit Commission (2006) www.areaprofiles.audit-commission.gov.uk/, accessed 6 December 2006.

Baldock, P. (1974) *Community Work and Social Work*. London: Routledge & Kegan Paul.

Christakopoulou, S., Dawson, J. and Gari, A. (2001) 'The community well-being questionnaire: theoretical context and initial assessment of its reliability and validity', *Social Indicators Research*, 56: 321–51.

Doyal, L. and Gough, I. (1991) *A Theory of Human Need*. Basingstoke: Macmillan.

Henderson, P. and Thomas, D.N. (1987) *Skills in Neighbourhood Work*. London: Routledge.

London Borough of Southwark (1987) *Fair Shares? The Southwark Poverty Profile*. London: London Borough of Southwark.

Merseyside County Council (1983) *The Closure of Smurfit Corrugated Cases Ltd.* Liverpool: Merseyside County Council.

Milson, F. (1974) *An Introduction to Community Work*. London: Routledge & Kegan Paul.

Newcastle City Council (1985) *Newcastle upon Tyne – A Social Audit*. Newcastle: Newcastle City Council.

New Economics Foundation (2006) www.neweconomics.org/gen/newways_socialaudit.aspx/ and www.proveandimprove.org/new/, accessed 31 October 2006.

Packham, C. (1998) 'Community auditing as community development', *Community Development Journal*, 33(3): 249–59.

Percy-Smith, J. (ed.) (1996) *Needs Assessments in Public Policy*. Buckingham: Open University Press.

Skinner, S. (1997) *Building Community Strengths: A Resource Book on Capacity Building*. London: Community Development Foundation.

Twelvetrees, A. (1991) *Community Work*. Basingstoke: Macmillan.

2   Why do a community profile?

Why might a community, voluntary organization or statutory agency want to construct a profile of a local community? There are a range of possible reasons that this chapter considers. Being clear about why you are undertaking a profile and the potential benefits that it could bring are important first steps in the planning process. We consider the reasons first from the point of view of communities and then from the point of view of statutory services and those responsible for planning and implementing public policies and programmes. However, in reality the reasons for profiling – and the benefits – are similar across both groups.

Since the 1960s various government policy initiatives have sought to address issues relating to communities. These initiatives have taken many forms and have been informed by a variety of competing values and philosophies (see Taylor 2003) but running through them have been a number of recurring themes including: the need for **'capacity building'** within communities; improvement of public services in disadvantaged communities especially through decentralized management; and the recognition of the importance of adopting holistic and integrated approaches to community development and neighbourhood renewal that address social, economic and physical aspects together rather than as single issues. Profiling the holistic needs of a community is reflective of these themes and is well expressed in the following quote:

> A comprehensive profile designed to facilitate effective urban policy initiatives should not just provide an understanding of the positive and negative elements of a local community but also contribute to an understanding of people's behaviour and how the community functions. For instance, it should not just examine people's perceptions of the sense of community but the type and scale of social interaction that takes place.
>
> (Christakopoulou *et al.* 2001).

Reasons for communities to profile

Community groups or groups of residents engage in community profiling exercises of one kind or another for a wide range of different reasons. The main ones are outlined in the following sections (see also Figure 2.1 for a summary of reasons). Of course, in many cases there will be a number of reasons for undertaking a community profile; Figure 2.2 (overleaf) shows the objectives for a community profile undertaken by a community development worker in North Somerset.

Research carried out by a community group can help to:
- assess the particular needs and wants of a group of people or a local community
- find out if people's needs are being met
- identify trends in services
- map existing local services and organizations and find out what others are doing
- monitor and evaluate a service or project

It can also help to:
- provide information for fundraising, lobbying or campaigning
- deliver services and activities in a way that is best for people
- prioritize and make best use of limited resources
- create a good relationship with those who use services
- encourage people to be involved in your group or organization
- promote your group or organization as open and accountable to users

---

Figure 2.1   Why do community groups need to do research?

Source: ARVAC (2001) *Community Research: Getting Started*. London: ARVAC: 2

To build understanding and community capacity

In some cases community profiles are used – especially by community workers and other professionals serving local areas – as an early step in the process of community development. The idea here is that through the process of undertaking the community profile local residents will become actively engaged in their community, will increase their awareness and understanding of the issues affecting their community, including its strengths, and will also acquire new skills and hopefully greater self-confidence. An example of this approach is the SCARF (Scottish Community Action Research Fund) project. Launched in Scotland in 2002 it provides grants to community organizations that want to develop skills to research their own needs and increase their effectiveness (see note on SCARF in Appendix 3).

- To inform members of the local community of community facilities at the Campus [building housing community facilities]
- To identify needs within the community
- To collate and represent information in a report, in order that consideration be given to how relevant agencies might work with the local community

Figure 2.2 Statement of intent for area profile, Locking Castle East, North Somerset

Source: North Somerset Council (2005) *Area Profile: Locking Castle East*: 7

If community capacity building is the primary reason for undertaking the community profile then the emphasis is likely to be very much on the profiling *process* rather than the end product. For a profiling exercise to provide the basis for this kind of community capacity building it will need to meet certain criteria. First, the community must be involved at all stages of the exercise (planning, design, fieldwork, data analysis and follow-up) and feel a sense of ownership of both the process and the outcomes (see Chapter 4 for a more detailed discussion of community involvement). This will, in turn, mean that sufficient time must be allowed for preparation and planning and the subsequent work will also have to take place at a pace that is right for the community members involved. (For an example of a community needs audit that aimed to develop the skills of members of the community see Figure 2.3.)

Second, the community profiling process will have to be designed in ways that provide plenty of opportunities for the members of the community involved to discuss ideas and options while at the same time keeping the project moving forwards. In addition mechanisms will need to be built in to the process to facilitate communication with, and feedback to, the wider community.

Third, the profiling process should go beyond an assessment of needs to

The aim of the Chapeltown and Harehills Community Needs Audit was to 'develop the skills within the community to provide quality research that gives real meaning to the expressed needs, fears and aspirations of Chapeltown and Harehills' diverse communities. The Community Development Foundation was commissioned to develop, from a community development perspective, an Open College Network accredited course.' The course trained local people in social research skills; armed with these skills they then undertook a community needs audit.

Figure 2.3 Example of a community needs audit that aimed to develop skills

Source: Leeds City Council (2000) *Getting to Know Your Community. Chapeltown and Harehills Community Needs Audit*. Leeds: Department of Housing and Environmental Health Services

become a positive exercise that identifies strengths and opportunities within the community and makes links and connections between issues.

Following on from the building of capacity, the development of skills and the raising of the awareness of community members of themselves as a community, a profile can also generate a desire for further action on the part of the community. For example, the community profiling exercise might have highlighted the isolation of lone parents with pre-school children in a local area. The community might then feel able to take action to address this issue through the development of a mums and tots session or play group.

In addition there has been a long tradition of practitioner-led community-based practitioner research, especially in relation to social care, library and information services, community health and youth and community work. Such research is, typically, undertaken in order to find out more about the needs of a local area, as a part of the process of familiarization with a locality for practitioners new in post or as a prelude to a new project or programme of work (see, for example, Fuller and Petch 1995). Figure 2.4 gives a description of a youth community profile that is designed to act as a 'planning tool' for youth workers.

A youth community profile is a planning tool for workers and contains a description of the local area, as it impacts on young people. It should contain information about the key features that shape a young person's experience and future. It includes both statistical evidence and qualitative information, gained from a variety of sources. It is likely to be written by an established worker with local knowledge, in conjunction with the area team, with young people and key partners.

Figure 2.4   Youth community profiles

Source: National Youth Agency, www.nya.org.uk/, accessed 6 December 2006

To support community campaigns

Voluntary organizations have used community profiling exercises as a means of demonstrating to service providers and statutory bodies that their community has needs that are not being met or that it lacks services or resources of a particular type. Community profiles have also been used as the basis for developing campaigns against particular local developments. Social audits in particular have been used in the past as a means of demonstrating the impact or effects of change on the quality of life of a community, notably the effects of closing a local factory or developing out-of-town retail parks. Furthermore there is a long and honourable tradition of using community-based research, including community profiles, to highlight issues of poverty and to underpin calls for social justice (see Green 2000). See Figures 2.5a and 2.5b for examples of community profiles carried out as part of a community campaign.

A community profile was commissioned by Govanhill Community Development Trust to provide it with information to enable the community to make its case for area regeneration, including greater coordination of effort and additional resources. The Report gave the Govanhill Community Development Trust a strategic overview of the main issues of community concern so that:

- Govanhill Community Development Trust could organize its work to match the priorities identified by the local community
- the lack of resources coming into the area can be clearly highlighted
- the case for a 'Govanhill Plan' can be clearly made

Figure 2.5a   Govanhill community profile

Source: Govanhill Community Development Trust (n.d.) *Govanhill Community Profile.* Glasgow: Govanhill Community Development Trust: 2, www.povertyalliance.org/html/resources/publications/GOVANHILL_pages.pdf

---

A community needs analysis was commissioned by the South Leeds Elderly Group – a community organization set up to cater for the needs of the Asian elderly in south Leeds. Existing services for elderly Asian residents were felt to be inadequate so a local survey was undertaken to assess the needs of Asian elders and their carers. The survey also enabled the group to identify gaps in current social services and health provision. A questionnaire was designed with assistance from Leeds Metropolitan University and fieldwork was undertaken by two local development workers and a number of trained volunteers. The findings from the survey gave rise to a series of recommendations for improvements in services in the area.

Figure 2.5b   The needs of Muslim elders and their carers in south Leeds

Source: South Leeds Elderly Group (1998) *Muslim Elders and Their Carers: Needs in the Community.* Leeds: South Leeds Elderly Group

To support funding applications

An increasingly important reason why communities engage in community profiling exercises is to support applications for funding of various kinds. Many grant-making bodies require organizations making applications to demonstrate that there is a need for the particular service or facility for which funding is being sought and how the proposal relates to existing services. For example, the application form for the Big Lottery Fund's (BLF) Community Buildings programme asks applicants to explain what the need is for the project being proposed and to say how that need was identified (Big Lottery Fund 2006).

In addition, applicants are asked to describe the people and organizations that are likely to benefit from the project and how they have been consulted. A community profile that focused on existing usage of community buildings and potential future uses would be a useful way of generating this kind of information. Many other funding regimes have similar requirements for information of this kind.

Statutory services and government programmes

Customer feedback

Some of the current interest in **community participation** and consultation has its roots in the 1980s and the Thatcher government's efforts to introduce a market approach to the delivery of public services. This included the need to be responsive to what the 'customer' wants and led to efforts to canvass customers' views. Some elements of this approach have been carried through to New Labour, in particular the focus on public involvement and participation as a means of making public services more accountable. Furthermore, New Labour's policy focus on **social exclusion** has also led to a recognition that disadvantaged communities typically face multiple, interrelated problems that are not amenable to a single-issue focus. This too has supported approaches that seek to build up a comprehensive and multifaceted picture of a community before engaging in action to tackle the problems.

Evidence-based policy and practice

More recently the evidence-based policy and practice movement has acted as a driver of community-based research. It has become an increasingly important tenet of contemporary policy that it should be 'evidence-based'; in other words, that policies should be informed by the best available research and evidence. This is reflected at the local level where it is often the case that local policy and practice has to be justified in terms of the evidence. This evidence might relate to needs, customers' or service users' views or the findings on 'what works' from evaluative studies and reviews. At the local level community profiles can provide a rich source of evidence on which to base plans for the future development of local services.

Statutory requirements

In some areas of local government there are specific statutory requirements to undertake research. In most cases these requirements are found in relation to the preparation of plans, strategies or policy statements. A recent report (Solesbury and Grayson 2003) identified both a number of areas in which there is a statutory duty to undertake research and also further areas where the necessity for research in fulfilling statutory requirements is not explicitly noted in the statute (see Figure 2.6). In both cases what is implied could involve community-based research of one kind or another.

- Review of housing needs (Housing Act 1985)
- Crime and disorder strategies (Crime and Disorder Act 1998)
- Community strategies (Local Government Act 2000)
- Early years development and childcare plans (School Standards and Framework Act 1998 as amended by the Education Act 2002)
- Accessibility strategies (Special Educational Needs and Disability Act 2001)
- Community care service plans (National Health Service and Community Care Act 1990)

Figure 2.6 Statutory requirements for research: examples that could lend themselves to a community profiling approach

Source: Solesbury and Grayson (2003)

Identifying and responding to needs and priorities for action

A key theme running through recent approaches to the delivery of public services is to identify and respond to local needs more effectively. This, it is argued, will result in better targeting of local services and more efficient deployment of resources. To this end many local authorities and other agencies have set up often sophisticated systems for analysing and sometimes mapping local administrative data. For example, the Housing Act 1985 requires local authorities to undertake a regular review of housing needs in the local area. Furthermore, an important part of the rationale for the Audit Commission's Area Profiles project (Audit Commission 2006) is to enable local public service providers to 'focus more clearly on the issues that most need improving locally'.

A central theme of the government's ten-year vision for local government is the engagement of more people in making decisions and setting priorities in localities and neighbourhoods. One aspect of this has been the proliferation of consultation exercises that seek to find out the views of local people on a wide range of topics including satisfaction with existing services and priorities for the future.

Using 'local knowledge' in service planning

In many areas of policy – including policing and community safety, environment, childcare – there has been a recognition that, far from the professionals or 'experts' always knowing best, their technical knowledge can be added to and enhanced through what can be seen as 'local knowledge'. In other words, the knowledge people gain from living and working in a community can offer insights that can affect the way in which services are delivered. As a result public agencies have tried to capture this local knowledge and apply it to the design and implementation of services. Related to this is the recognition that the evaluation of programmes and projects should also take account of the views of beneficiaries and other stakeholders.

The perceptions of service users – and especially those who might themselves constitute discrete 'communities' such as users of mental health services, or people with disabilities, or people with a learning disability, or carers – have become particularly important in relation to the development and delivery of health and social care services. As a result there have been numerous local consultations with user groups in order to tap into their specialist local knowledge.

Providing a baseline against which to measure future progress

Part of the agenda of the modernization of public services has been the increased emphasis on accountability of public services. As a consequence a wide range of indicators and measures have been developed for assessing the performance of public agencies and reporting on that performance to the general public. This has been the case in relation to Best Value, education, and to local authorities more generally through the Comprehensive Performance Assessment rating. All these performance indicators and measures are underpinned by research and/or data-gathering exercises of one kind or another.

Government policy initiatives

In addition to these cross-cutting reasons for undertaking community-based research, a number of more specific recent policy initiatives also have implications for community-based research. However, it has been argued that not all of these exercises contribute unambiguously to community participation or empowerment (see Jones and Jones 2002).

Sustainable communities

Since the Local Government Act 2000 local authorities in England and Wales have been required to draw up a **community strategy** for the local area, setting out a shared long-term vision which combines economic, environmental and social objectives. In Scotland **community plans** are undertaken under the auspices of the Local Government in Scotland Act 2003. This community planning process is led by the local authority but undertaken together with a wide range of local partners, usually through **Local Strategic Partnerships**. The Community Strategies guidance stresses the importance of engaging and involving local communities and of undertaking a proper assessment of needs and resource availability (DETR 2000).

This process has recently been embedded still further through the 2006 Local Government White Paper (DCLG 2006a), which reinforces the role of the local authority together with partners in developing Sustainable Community Strategies. A further element in the government's strategy for localities is to empower people to get involved in a wide range of activities at the neighbourhood level (DCLG 2006b). An important part of the sustainable communities strategy is to use evidence – about local needs and priorities – to provide the rationale for local planning.

Community planning exercises are also taking place at other levels including the parish and the market town. Agencies such as the Countryside Agency have been instrumental in encouraging such initiatives (see Countryside Agency 2002) and the Quality Parish Councils scheme includes in its criteria that parish and town councils should 'articulate the needs and wishes of the community'. As a result the last ten years have seen a proliferation of **village and parish appraisals**.

Neighbourhood renewal

The government's approach to neighbourhood renewal as set out in successive documents since 2001 has included a recognition that systematically assessing local areas is an important early stage in the neighbourhood renewal process and that the success of an area-based approach is likely to be affected by the extent to which it is based on a thorough understanding of the local area. For example, in relation to housing renewal, the reasons for undertaking a local assessment are clearly articulated in the guidance (see Figure 2.7).

The *National Strategy for Neighbourhood Renewal* (Social Exclusion Unit 2000) set out wide-ranging plans to address the needs of people living in the most disadvantaged areas. Two programmes are particularly important in this context. The first is New Deal for Communities (NDC), which has as a central plank the idea that the regeneration activities undertaken under the auspices of the programme should be overseen by a board on which local residents are represented and, furthermore, the programme should be developed in response to the identified needs of the local community. This led to detailed analyses of local needs in the NDC areas including work with local communities to identify priorities. The second programme is Neighbourhood Management; the central idea behind this approach is that mainstream services can be 'bent' so that they are delivered in ways that more effectively

- It will provide the context to understand the socio-economic and environmental factors influencing the area
- It will ensure that investment decisions are taken into account based on an in-depth knowledge of the local neighbourhood
- It will provide a transparent framework for communicating the process of investment decisions with all stakeholders
- It will ensure that policy is evidence-based
- It should encourage greater integration between housing activities and other activities
- Detailed understanding of the issues should lead to better service delivery

Figure 2.7   Why should you undertake a neighbourhood renewal assessment?

Source: ODPM (2004) *Neighbourhood Renewal Assessment. Guidance Manual 2004.* London: ODPM

meet the needs of local people, especially those who live in disadvantaged areas. The aim is to put local services under the management of a single individual or team at the neighbourhood level. In so doing, Neighbourhood Management also seeks to harness the knowledge of local people so that they have more say in the provision of local services. An understanding of local needs is therefore crucial to the success of neighbourhood management.

Summary of key issues

Community profiles have made useful contributions to policy and practice in the past and continue to serve a number of useful functions. Indeed, they are very much in tune with significant strands of current and recent government policy. These include the need for policies and programmes and local statutory services to show that they are identifying and responding to local needs and priorities; requirements for accountability and to demonstrate effectiveness in service delivery; and the development of a more holistic approach to addressing social disadvantage. These themes are perhaps best reflected in two major initiatives: the requirement on local authorities to undertake local community strategies or plans and the national strategy for neighbourhood renewal. Community profiles are making important contributions to these initiatives and programmes.

More important than community profiles undertaken by statutory agencies or in response to government programmes are those profiles undertaken by or with community organizations. Typically these are undertaken as part of a broader programme of community development within a local area and are designed to build community capacity, confidence and skills so that the community is better able to take action for itself. In addition, community profiles are used by community organizations to underpin bids for funding or to apply pressure for more or better services to meet local needs.

References

Audit Commission (2006) www.areaprofiles.audit-commission.gov.uk/, accessed 6 December 2006.

Big Lottery Fund (2006) www.biglotteryfund.org.uk/prog_community_buildings/, accessed 6 December 2006.

Christakopoulou, S., Dawson, J. and Gari, A. (2001) 'The community well-being questionnaire: theoretical context and initial assessment of its reliability and validity', *Social Indicators Research*, 56: 321–51.

Countryside Agency (2002) *Parish Plans – Guidance for Parish and Town Councils*. Cheltenham: Countryside Agency.

DCLG (Department for Communities and Local Government) (2006a) *Strong and Prosperous Communities*, Cm 6939. London: The Stationery Office.

DCLG (2006b) *Citizen Engagement and Public Services: Why Neighbourhoods Matter*. London: The Stationery Office.

DETR (Department of the Environment, Transport and the Regions) (2000) *Preparing Community Strategies: Government Guidance to Local Authorities*. London: The Stationery Office.

Fuller, R. and Petch, A. (1995) *Practitioner Research: The Reflexive Social Worker*. Buckingham: Open University Press.

Green, R. (2000) 'Applying a community needs profiling approach to tackling service user poverty', *British Journal of Social Work*, 30: 287–303.

Jones, J. and Jones, L. (2002) 'Research and citizen participation', *Journal of Community Work and Development*, 1(3): 50–66.

Social Exclusion Unit (2000) *A National Strategy for Neighbourhood Renewal: A Consultation Document*. London: The Stationery Office.

Solesbury, W. and Grayson, L. (2003) *Statutory Requirements for Research: A Review of Responsibilities for English and Welsh Local Government*. London: LGA/LARIA.

Taylor, M. (2003) *Public Policy in the Community*. Basingstoke: Palgrave.

3 Planning a community profile

Having decided to do a community profile the next step must be to plan the work. This is a vital part of the process and failure to spend sufficient time on it is likely to lead to difficulties later. This chapter takes you through the steps that you ideally need to include in your plan, as shown in Figure 3.1 (overleaf), and discusses in detail the issues and options associated with the first two stages of community profiling, which we have called 'Preparing the ground' and 'Setting aims and objectives'. These stages, along with deciding on methods (Chapter 5), are the planning and decision-making elements of the profiling process and, for that reason, are discussed in detail in this chapter. The stages of the profiling process concerned with information gathering, data analysis, presentation of findings and action planning are discussed in detail in subsequent chapters.

Preparing the ground

At the very beginning of your project, you will probably have a plan to do a profile of a particular community, a few interested people and some preliminary ideas about issues that you want to examine. In order to take the profile forward from the ideas stage to the practical work stage, there are a number of different tasks that will need to be accomplished. They are all important, since they will, in large part, set the tone for your future work, its scope and your style of working. The order in which these tasks are undertaken is less important than that they should all be accomplished.

Creating a steering group

Chapter 4 emphasizes the importance of involving a wide range of stakeholders in the community profiling process, therefore one of the very first tasks that you need to undertake is to get additional people involved through

Preparing the ground
- Creating a steering group
- Initial planning
- Making contacts
- Learning from others' experiences
- Identifying resources
- Engaging consultants or professional researchers
- Developing a management structure

Setting aims and objectives

Deciding on methods

Fieldwork
- Production of information-gathering tools, e.g. questionnaires
- Training of staff involved in data collection
- Collecting 'new' information
- Recording information
- Analysing information

Reporting
- Writing up fieldwork
- Production of draft profile
- Consultations on draft profile
- Amendments to draft profile
- Production of final community profile
- Dissemination of research findings

Action
- Consultations over key issues, priorities, action to be taken
- Drafting community action plan
- Consultations over draft plan
- Production of action plan
- Dissemination of action plan
- Implementation
- Monitoring and evaluation

Figure 3.1 Stages in the community profiling process

setting up a project steering group. How much work you have to do in order to develop a project steering group may depend on how the idea to do a community profile came about. It may be the case that you already have a dedicated group of people who are committed to the idea. If not, then you will have to create such a group of people who will direct and organize the early stages of the work until such time as decisions are taken about how the project is to be managed. The ideal size for a steering group will vary considerably between projects and will depend on the size of the community, the scope of the profile to be undertaken and the time and dedication of those involved. It might be as small as two or three committed and energetic people or as large as 12 or 13. Whatever the number, the group must be small enough to work effectively but large enough that interested people are not excluded. Chapter 4 includes some additional ideas about involving stakeholders in this stage of the project.

There are a number of ways in which you might go about assembling a group of people to form a steering group. The aim is to recruit people who share a commitment to the idea but who come from a variety of different organizations (even if the project is led, by necessity, by one agency), or who represent different sections within the community, or who are likely to offer a range of different perspectives so that the project is not dominated from the outset by a particular viewpoint. One way to do this is to organize a public meeting in an appropriate venue which is widely publicized and indicate that all are welcome to come. A potential problem with this approach is that you have no idea at all who, if anyone, will turn up and whether they have any real understanding of what you are trying to achieve.

An alternative approach might be to write a letter setting out what you want to do and why and send it to as many groups and individuals as possible in the community in which you are interested, inviting them to come to a meeting. Examples of some of the groups and organizations you might wish to contact are listed in Figure 3.2 (overleaf). Of course, the kinds of groups who you get in touch with will vary according to whether you are profiling a geographical community or a group of people sharing common characteristics. If you are doing the former, then you will want to invite representatives from the statutory services who work in that community; if you are doing the latter, you may wish to invite a person who has special responsibility for developing or providing services for that particular group. For example, if you are profiling women in your city, then you may want to invite local authority departments to send an officer who has special responsibility for services for women and any group or organization that campaigns on women's issues.

In addition, you may want to invite representatives of groups who have resources of various kinds which you may wish to make use of, such as your local Council for Voluntary Services, which may be a useful starting point for building up contacts, or anyone with an interest in community development or social science research methods at your local university.

In general, you are more likely to get a positive response if you can send your invitation to a named individual rather than to the organization. If it has gone to the 'wrong' person, then they are quite likely to pass it on to a more

Statutory services
- Adult care services
- Early years
- Children's services
- Supporting people
- Housing and homelessness services
- Police
- Library
- Leisure/sports centre
- Local schools
- Further and higher education establishments in the area
- Planning department
- Health centre
- Youth services

Voluntary/community organizations
- Tenants'/residents' group
- Black and minority ethnic groups
- Neighbourhood association
- Faith groups
- Elderly persons' luncheon club
- Campaigning groups, e.g. Age Concern, Shelter, Gingerbread, Mencap

Partnership organizations
- Local Strategic Partnerships
- Area-based initiatives such as New Deal for Communities or Sure Start

Community representatives
- Ward councillors (parish, district/city, county)
- MP
- MEP
- Other community 'leaders' and representatives of area committees and forums

Commercial representatives
- Local shops
- Employers whose workforce may be primarily from the community

Figure 3.2   Examples of individuals, groups and organizations to invite to the initial steering group meeting

appropriate person. When you write to these individuals, groups and organizations, it is a good idea to include a tear-off slip asking people to indicate whether they will be attending and, if not, whether they would like to be kept informed of progress.

At the meeting, you will need to set out clearly what it is you are trying to do and why, and explain the purpose of the meeting. By the end of the meeting, you should aim to have achieved all the objectives listed in Figure 3.3. This is more than enough to do at the first meeting! However, try to arrange the next meeting for a date fairly soon after, as you still have a lot of work to do before the steering group can really function effectively. At the next meeting, you may find yourself concentrating on the group itself and how it should work. There are a number of issues which need to be addressed, as shown in Figure 3.4. This may be a time-consuming discussion, but it is especially important if the steering group is also to be the project management group. If, however, the steering group intends to hand over to a different project management group at a later date, then you may feel that some of these issues are best left until later. Having addressed these issues, the group is then in a position to move on to the more substantive issues of relevance to the profile.

- Reach a shared understanding of what, in broad terms, the project is about
- Gain a view about the extent to which people think it is a good idea (if not many people are in favour, you may need to go away and think again!)
- Obtain a commitment from a group of those present to constitute themselves as a steering group
- Agree the terms of reference of the steering group
- Identify the next steps that need to be taken
- Agree a time and place for the next meeting

Figure 3.3 Objectives of initial steering group meeting

- Is the steering group as it is presently constituted an appropriate size?
- Are there other people whom you need to get on board at this stage?
- How often will the group meet?
- Who will be responsible for convening meetings?
- Will there be an agenda and minutes? If so, who is responsible for drawing them up?
- Who is allowed to have access to these documents?
- Is there to be a chairperson? If not, how will meetings be organized/coordinated?
- Where will the group meet?

Figure 3.4 Organization of the steering group

There are six tasks that need to be accomplished quite quickly. These are: initial planning, including preliminary identification of the community and issues to be covered by the profile; making contact with relevant community groups, leaders and key actors; learning from others' experience; identifying available resources; engaging consultants or professional researchers; and the development of a management structure. We shall look in turn at what each of these entails. You might want to assign responsibility for the completion of these tasks to different members of the steering group, so that the burden of work is shared, and also to maintain commitment and enthusiasm on the part of group members.

Initial planning

At this point in the process, you will have an effectively functioning group with an idea or several ideas. The next task is to refine those ideas into something workable. The first important decision that you have to make is what exactly is the community that is going to be profiled. If you are interested in a geographically located community, then it is useful to start off with a street map of the whole area. Begin by marking any 'natural' boundaries to the community such as parks, railway lines, motorways or major roads. This may identify some boundaries but is unlikely to identify all of them. There are at least three other relevant considerations which may help you define your community. The first is commonly held local views about where the community or neighbourhood begins or ends. The second is whether there are any administrative boundaries that cut across your area. It is always easier to work with data that relates to the boundaries you are working with. The most obvious administrative boundaries which you may want to draw in on your map are Output Areas, Polling Districts and statutory service administrative boundaries such as health, housing and social services. In practice, these rarely coincide with each other, but it is important to at least know where they are. The final consideration is to define your community in such a way that it is manageable in terms of size.

If, on the other hand, your chosen community is a 'community of interest', for example women, an ethnic group or young people, you may still have to make decisions about boundaries. For example: are you going to include women from throughout the district or city or just one part of the city? What age groups are you going to include in the category 'young people'? Exactly which ethnic group are you interested in? A further consideration is how you intend to identify your community. (There is further information on how to structure a sample in Appendix 2.)

A further task to be accomplished as part of this initial planning is to identify a preliminary list of issues that you want to examine as part of the community profile. For example, is your profile intended to be comprehensive,

covering most issues that affect people such as health, housing, the environment, employment, welfare services, education, childcare, transport and so
on? Or are you focusing on a more limited range of issues such as skills, training and employment, or needs and resources in relation to welfare provision?
At this stage, you should regard this list of issues as provisional, pending
consultations with a wider group.

Making contacts

Now you are in a position to begin to develop contacts within the community
that you have identified and begin some initial consultation about the scope
of the profile. You should already have begun to compile a list of key individuals and organizations within your community and the steering group
should now add to this. Having compiled as complete a list as possible, you
then need to inform them about the project, seek their support and cooperation, and arrange to talk to as many people as possible. The first step in this
process is likely to be the sending out of a letter giving details of the project,
inviting comments and/or suggesting that the letter will be followed up within
a week or so with a telephone call to arrange a meeting to discuss the project
further. You may not have the resources or the time to see all these groups and
individuals at this stage; if not, make sure that you have at least contacted the
people whom you think are the most important community 'gatekeepers' (for
example, representatives of ethnic minority community associations in areas
where the ethnic minority population is significant) and a cross-section of
others, for example some representatives of voluntary, community and statutory organizations, some elected community representatives and so on. If you
do have to prioritize who to see, then be aware of the politics of your community. There may be groups or individuals who will take offence if they are
not consulted at this early stage.

Rather than talking only to representatives or leaders of groups (who may
not be truly representative), it might be a better idea to contact groups like
mother and toddler groups, tenant associations and so on, and ask if you
can have a half-hour 'slot' at some point during their next meeting to explain
the project, and invite questions, comments, suggestions and offers of
help. One of the aims of this series of meetings is to add to and amend your
initial list of issues and to identify 'resources' (see the section on 'Identifying
resources' on page 30).

Learning from others' experience

A further task that can usefully be carried out at this stage is to find out
whether anyone else has tried to do something similar to what you are
planning to do and whether there are any other major pieces of community

development work planned for your area. If you have made contact with all the agencies and groups listed in Figure 3.2 you should have a good idea about this; however, you can also supplement this knowledge with an internet search. In addition, Councils for Voluntary Services often have copies of profiles relating to their area and Citizens Advice Bureau workers, health visitors and community nurses sometimes have to draw up a local profile as part of their training. Talking to other people who have undertaken a similar exercise to your own before you start work can enable you to learn from their experience and, hopefully, avoid any mistakes which they may have made.

Identifying resources

Any community profiling exercise relies for its success on having a quite extensive range of resources. It is very important to have a clear understanding of three issues in relation to resources. What resources does the group already have or have access to? What resources does the group need but does not have at the moment? Which of these are vital for the successful completion of the project and how can they be obtained? You might want to draw up a grid along the lines indicated in Figure 3.5 (opposite) to help with this process.

Some external sources of assistance which you may want to consider using are staff from:

- your local university or college of further education, who may be able to offer help with survey design and data analysis;
- a community resource centre, who may be able to provide assistance with printing and photocopying;
- your local Planning Department, who may be willing to supply maps free of charge;
- your local library, who will help you track down documents relating to your community.

Engaging consultants or professional researchers

Depending on the financial resources which you have available and the expertise that you have within your group, you may want to engage consultants or professional researchers to undertake all or part of the work for you. Since this book is aimed principally at those intending to carry out most of the work themselves, we do not discuss this in detail. However, the Social Research Association (SRA) has produced good practice guidelines on commissioning social research (Social Research Association 2002) and your local Council for Voluntary Services may be able to help you find an appropriate organization to assist you. However, it is worth saying that engaging profes-

Resource	Available from within group	Vital to success of project (Y/N)	Can be obtained from ...?
Person power			
Money			
Design skills			
Computing skills			
Research skills			
Interview skills			
Group work skills			
Computer			
Internet			
Photocopier			
Maps			
Local contacts			

Figure 3.5   Resources grid

sional researchers or consultants will itself entail considerable work. You will have to draw up a project specification setting out what the project is about, what you require the consultants to do, any ideas you have about the methods to be used or the style of working you would prefer, the contractual arrangements and how they should 'bid' for the work if you are approaching more than one organization. Having appointed researchers you will then have to write a contract specifying in detail the work to be done, the timescale, the amount to be paid and when and how they are to report to you. In addition, you will have to work out a means of managing the consultants so that you have the amount of input into the work that you want, for example over the design of questionnaires or the wording of press releases. It can be very disappointing to spend a large amount of money on a piece of work carried out by professional researchers or consultants only to discover that they have not really done what you wanted them to do or they are not working in the way that you had expected. An alternative is to pay a professional researcher or consultant for, say, a day's worth of advice on questionnaire design or data analysis.

Developing a management structure

At some point during this initial 'preparing-the-ground' stage, you will have to make a decision about how the project should be managed. It may be appropriate for the steering group simply to continue as the project management group. This is probably satisfactory if you are confident that the steering group contains a cross-section of representatives of the community and, more importantly, has credibility with that community. Having the 'right' people on board at the beginning can increase ownership and the likelihood that the profile will be used. If this is not the case, however, you will probably need to create a new management group to take the project forward. If the management group is going to have credibility with the community, then its appointment will have to occur at a public meeting which all members of, and stakeholders in, the community are invited to attend. You might also want to use this meeting to formally launch the community profiling project with appropriate publicity. The meeting should be advertised widely using all or some of the following methods: posters and/or leaflets displayed in the library, health centre, social services office, housing office, community centre, leisure centre, etc.; letters sent to community groups, voluntary organizations, community representatives and leaders inviting them to attend; press release sent to local newspapers; item included in 'open space' slot in local radio or television programme.

Having brought people together in this way, the steering group should explain to those attending what the project is about, what progress has been made to date and what the meeting is for. The main purpose of the meeting is to seek cooperation and support and elect, nominate or appoint a management committee. Whatever method you choose, you should bear in mind the fact that some people may be reluctant to put themselves forward, so you may need to encourage people to nominate others and possibly leave yourselves the option of co-opting people if you think that you have not got enough nominations or those that are being put forward are not drawn from a wide enough cross-section of the community.

In inviting nominations you need to make it clear what being a member of the management committee will entail in terms of the timing and frequency of meetings, other work that might be expected of them, and so on. In addition, you need to consider the kinds of things that act as barriers to people who might like to be involved and how these might be overcome. The issues that you might consider include: the accessibility of the venue for meetings; the times when meetings are held; childcare; and whether the way in which meetings are structured, organized and conducted is off-putting. However, it is also important that if the group promises to address particular barriers to participation they can deliver on the promise; in other words, if there is a commitment to provide assistance with childcare or babysitting, that there are appropriate resources available to back that commitment.

Another consideration in constructing the management committee is the size of the group. What is an appropriate size will depend in part on what you want the management committee to do. The committee needs to be large enough to provide sufficient people to undertake the work that has to be done but small enough to act as an effective decision-making body. In general, it is better to include everybody who wants to be involved as it is likely to cause bad feeling if some members of the community are excluded having put themselves forward and, anyway, some people will drop out over the course of the project.

Once a management committee has been appointed and some preliminary issues relating to timing and venues for meetings have been addressed, another meeting needs to be arranged quite quickly to which someone needs to bring a short draft paper setting out the terms of reference for the committee. These terms of reference should address the following issues:

- the membership of the management committee and whether this is fixed or open;
- the aims of the committee;
- how committee meetings are to be organized and any rules of working.

The management committee should now be in a position to take over the running of the project from the steering group and it must now address the crucial question of what the aims and objectives of the project are going to be.

Setting aims and objectives

The aims and objectives of the community profiling project will depend in large part on the overall purpose for which the profile is being carried out. In most cases, the profile will not be an end in itself but a means to an end. The aims and objectives that the group decides on must be clearly stated, quite specific and must be agreed to by the whole management group. It is important that the reason for doing the profile is kept in mind so that others do not attach their own objectives to the project, making it too unwieldy. It may be that the list of objectives that is produced is too long to be manageable. If this is the case, then you will need to decide on priorities. Again, keeping the overall purpose in mind will help to focus on what the priorities ought to be.

Overall project planning

Chapter 5 explores all the relevant considerations when deciding on the methods to use in collecting information. However, at the same time that you are considering these methods you will need to consider the timescale for the project and any externally imposed time constraints such as deadlines for the submission of funding applications, local authority committee cycles and so on. The timetable should reflect what you are going to do, the resources available to you and how long you think it will take to build up relationships with people in the community. Don't forget to allow for holidays that might interrupt work on the project. In general, you need to allow sufficient time to enable the work to be done properly but without dragging the process out over such a long period of time that people lose interest. In most cases, you will need between four and six months to do a profile from start to finish, although this will vary according to the particular circumstances of your project. In planning a timetable it is useful to start by listing each of the separate tasks that need to be completed and to identify which of them have to be completed in order for the next stage to begin and which can run alongside each other. You should then be able to divide the project up into stages and set deadlines for the completion of each stage.

This is the end of the planning stage of the profile. By now you should be able to 'tick' all the items listed in Figure 3.6.

- A *management committee* with clear terms of reference, roles and responsibilities
- Consensus about the *purpose* of the community profile
- Consensus about the *community* to be profiled
- A preliminary list of *issues* to be addressed by the profile
- A clearly stated set of *aims and objectives*
- *Resources* that are appropriate to the task in hand
- *Contacts* within the community to be profiled

Figure 3.6 Checklist of things to be achieved by the end of the 'preparing-the-ground' stage

Summary of key issues

Spending time planning your community profile may seem to be time wasted that could usefully be spent getting on with the job. While it is important not to get too bogged down in planning at the expense of action, taking some time at the beginning of a project to think carefully and creatively about what you are trying to achieve and building up contacts and cooperation with the community is time well spent and could save time later. Many research projects ultimately fail either to be completed or to achieve their objectives because insufficient time was spent at the planning stage.

This chapter has focused on moving from an idea in the minds of a few individuals to do a community profile, through the creation of a small project steering group, to the setting up of a management committee. It has also taken the reader through the process of identifying preliminary issues, formulating aims and objectives, mobilizing resources and planning a timetable. In Chapter 4 we will consider how to go about involving the community and other stakeholders. It will look at one further aspect of the planning process in more detail – that is deciding on the methods to use.

References

Social Research Association (2002) *Commissioning Social Research. A Good Practice Guide*. London: Social Research Association, www.the-sra.org.uk/documents/pdfs/commissioning.pdf, accessed 6 December 2006.

4 Involving communities and other stakeholders

Community-based research has not always entailed the active involvement of the community being studied. However, enabling members of the community to participate in the community profiling process is likely to result in a more accurate and complete description. Furthermore, we would argue that members of a community have a right to be heard and to know what is being said about them. This chapter starts by looking at why communities and other stakeholders should be involved and the benefits of that involvement.

In community profiling 'the community' is used as an essential unit of identification, but what exactly do we mean by community? In this chapter, we look at this over-used, often hackneyed concept, including who might constitute the community. We then explore who, besides the community, might be 'stakeholders' in a community profile and important issues relating to the control and 'ownership' of the community profile raised by the involvement of stakeholders.

A central thesis of this book is that community profiles can be used to assist in the process of building the capacity of, and empowering, communities (see Chapter 2). In this chapter, we examine the various *levels* of community involvement, both in terms of the relative involvement of community members on the one hand and professionals or external helpers on the other, and also in terms of the *extent* of involvement individuals might have in the profiling process.

That process, as is shown in Figure 3.1 in the preceding chapter, comprises a number of stages from the initial idea to undertake a profile through to using the findings. The community and other stakeholders can be centrally involved in all those stages either directly or indirectly. Individuals may not always be able or willing to become involved and encouraging full involvement is not always easy. We therefore also include practical suggestions for maximizing involvement.

Why involve the community?

Interest in, and development of, involvement in governance for local service planning and delivery as well as in local research and practice has been growing steadily over the last decade. Since the late 1990s a series of programmes and projects has been initiated which aim at devolving far more decision making in the public sector to communities. As we have described in Chapter 2, the government have issued a series of policy documents that advocate involving communities and other partners in service planning and delivery. This development has gone some way towards recognizing the values of involving not only communities in decisions being made about them, but also a wide range of other stakeholders.

It is now widely acknowledged that to involve communities in the decision-making process it is necessary, over a period of time, for them to develop sufficient resources and knowledge about the relevant issues and context, and also the capacity to organize and make decisions. Community profiling is one of the key tools available to community workers working with communities in this way. The community profiling process itself can be used to promote co-learning and develop new skills and knowledge, and can even lead to an increase in resources for a community – in other words, build community capacity. Traditional research methods may provide an 'objective' (often sanitized) view of a community; however, as we will see later in this chapter, community development values imply that there is a duty to empower communities. This can be furthered not only by involving local residents but also by ensuring that they take ownership of the process. As those who are most closely involved in the processes are those who stand to benefit the most, it is therefore important to involve as many members of the community as possible in the community profile.

There are additional reasons for involving a wide range of other stakeholders. An inclusive and **participatory approach** to profiling can result in the collection of better quality and more robust information. It can help to ensure that the research is firmly rooted in 'the real world', focused on a local agenda with specific local concerns and issues, and steered in the direction of local needs and aspirations. It will also help to build the necessary trust with the researchers and to overcome suspicion and the effects of being continually, but often ineffectually, 'consulted'.

The idea of community

The idea of 'community' as a unit of identity is essential to understanding the whole profiling process as well as involvement and participation in that process. It is a term that has become almost impossible to define precisely as its usage has become so pervasive in our everyday language that its meaning is overlaid with a host of associations (European Community, **faith community**, community policing, community service), emotions (community charge, caring community, community spirit) and ideologies (communitarianism, community action). Indeed, Stacey (1969) argued that as the concept of community was used as a catch-all term to refer to almost any social groupings outside the confines of the family, it was so vague and 'mythical' as to be virtually useless. Similarly Hillery (1955: 117ff.) noted 94 separate definitions of community, commenting that the only thing they had in common was people. Hillery's list also showed that the definitions fell broadly into two categories: 'community' can be used to categorize and identify physical and geographic characteristics of human settlements or localities as well as to analyse and describe the nature and quality of the social relationships sustained by the community. After Stacey had declared the concept of community a 'myth', research came to be increasingly focused on location.

It is arguably the case that ever since the development of urban populations following industrialization, people have harked back to an idyllic, but probably imaginary, village community where everyone knew each other and interacted in a range of roles (working, worshipping, socializing, quarrelling) as compared to the alienating life of the city. In an attempt to revive 'community' as a meaningful concept for the modern world, Etzioni defines the term with reference to two characteristics: 'a web of affect-laden relationships among a group of people', and 'a measure of commitment to a shared set of values, norms, and meanings and a shared history and identity – in short, to a particular culture' (Etzioni 1996: 127). This view of community has been criticized for being prescriptive and over-emphasizing the role of the 'moral voice' in communities. Nevertheless communitarianism, as Etzioni's ideas were referred to, was attractive to New Labour and others because of its emphasis on public responsibility and civic duty.

What is the community?

Although the term 'community' is problematic it is nevertheless in everyday use not only by politicians but also professionals and practitioners and also by people living in those communities. In this book we use the term loosely to refer to a group of people related to each other through a common bond. A primary common bond is the place where people live. A geographical or locational community can range in size from a single street to an estate, neighbourhood, ward or other smaller administrative area such as a school catchment area, to a parish, village, town, district and, for some purposes, even counties, nations or groups of nations. Many boundaries used by statutory bodies to organize the delivery of services or the collection of information do not coincide with each other. Also, residents in a neighbourhood may them-selves define the boundary to their community differently. It is therefore important that when undertaking a community profile you agree initially with all stakeholders the precise boundaries of the area concerned.

There are other characteristics besides location that people have in com-mon that might lead to a sense of community. These might include age, gender, ethnicity or nationality. Other common bonds that can create a sense of belonging might include having a shared problem such as a medical condition or disability (visually impaired community), a shared working environment (miners' community), belonging to a particular faith (Catholic community), or being a member of a voluntary or political organization or alliance (Greenpeace community). These definitions are not, of course, mutu-ally exclusive and it is possible to undertake a profile using several of these characteristics. Again, it is important that everyone involved is clear on the definition and characteristics of the community to be profiled.

Definitions of community are almost always positive, evoking feelings of warmth and closeness. However, although there are no doubt communities like this, in many cases real efforts have to be made to develop a 'community spirit'. An idealized view can hide the reality that communities are not always comfortable or homogeneous; many communities contain underlying ten-sions and conflicts. They may be cross-cut by divisions – for example, race, gender and class – and contain groups whose interests conflict with each other. In the most divided communities these conflicts may be played out violently or through other forms of anti-social behaviour. It is therefore important to iden-tify clearly any overt or underlying conflicts within a community. You should try to ensure that the views of all factions are heard and that representatives of all sections of the community have an equal opportunity to take part in the process. Chapter 7 explores some of the practical issues related to engaging those groups who are marginalized or 'hard to reach'. Failure to involve such groups will not only produce an incomplete picture of the community but could also antagonize the under-represented section and exacerbate divisions.

Other stakeholders

In most communities there are other stakeholders in addition to the people who live there. In undertaking a community profile it is important to consider the full range of people who might have an interest or something to say. So, for example, in a spatially defined community profile you might include the views of those who represent the community in some way such as politicians (councillors, MPs and MEPs) and also members of trusts and boards, for instance New Deal for Communities Boards, School Governing Bodies, Primary Care Trusts and Registered Social Landlords.

Another category of stakeholders who have an interest in the community are those who work there but do not necessarily live as part of it. This group would include those whose place of work just happens to be in the locality, those who work for the community (doctors, teachers, police, street wardens, clergy and so on), and those who not only work for the community but are also more directly accountable to it (such as community workers, community regeneration officers and patch social workers). Businesses are also important parts of communities. Business representatives may be from large industrial sites located in or near the community that impact on residents, or from small and medium-sized enterprises, some of which may include local retailers such as local shops, post offices, take-away establishments and pubs.

In addition to representatives from the statutory and business sectors you will also want to involve voluntary, community and faith organizations that work in your area to provide services, self-help, or to lobby or campaign on behalf of the community or particular groups within it.

Involving non-resident stakeholders

Involving non-resident stakeholders carries some risks in so far as the community profile is part of a community development process. A particular issue here is who has overall control of the process. This relates to how the community is seen and sees itself. For example, Haggstrom, whose work informed the development of community work in the 1970s, argued that communities have two guises: community as *object* and *acting community* (Haggstrom 1970). The first can be seen as a network of interdependent systems, bureaucratic organizations, interest groups, political parties and so on that is acted upon. Acting communities, on the other hand, identify their own needs and problems, participate in decision making and engage in collective action.

Many stakeholders 'act on' communities, often in an expert capacity, believing that it is in the community's best interest. However, they may unwittingly behave in a patronizing way, creating dependency and the very state of apathy that so many of them deplore. To combat such attitudes a community development approach evolved in the 1970s that incorporated a different set of beliefs and values. In this approach community development is not seen as just a means to another end but as an end in itself – that is, empowering residents. The community development approach incorporates the belief that 'acting communities' can lead to liberation, development and fulfilment through cooperation, shared interests and values. Community profiles can contribute to this process by not only focusing on needs, issues and problems but also by recognizing, celebrating and building on the strengths and resources of all the community.

More recently, in 2002 the Community Work Forum, a grouping of employers, trades unions, training providers and practitioners, produced revised standards and definitions for community development work. These National Occupational Standards for Community Development Work are outlined in Figure 4.1 and exemplify the values and principles underpinning community work.

If a community profile is going to contribute to the community development process then it is necessary to develop a strategy for involving non-resident stakeholders that is informed by a consistent set of values and principles. In particular this strategy should address issues of purpose, ownership, direction and perception of the process by the community. One way of conceptualizing the relative control and degree of ownership by members of the community as opposed to non-resident stakeholders is to see the community profiling project as either a top-down exercise, where the profile is essentially carried out by outsiders with perhaps some consultation with

---

The key purpose of community development work is collectively to bring about social change and justice, by working with communities to:

- identify their needs, opportunities, rights and responsibilities
- plan, organize and take action
- evaluate the effectiveness and impact of the action
- and to do all these in ways which challenge oppression and tackle inequalities

Community work values

Social justice
Working towards a fairer society that respects civil and human rights and challenges oppression

Self-determination
Individuals and groups have the right to identify shared issues and concerns as the starting point for collective action

Working and learning together
Valuing and using the skills, knowledge, experience and diversity within communities to collectively bring about change

Sustainable communities
Empowering communities to develop their independence and autonomy whilst making and maintaining links to the wider society

Participation
Everyone has the right to fully participate in the decision-making processes that affect their lives

Reflective practice
Effective community development is informed and enhanced through reflection on action

---

Figure 4.1   Values associated with community development work

Source: From the definition of community development work by the Federation for Community Development Learning, www.fcdl.org.uk/publications/documents/sharing_practice_sheets/1_What_is_CD.pdf

community leaders, or as a bottom-up exercise, where the community itself takes charge of the profiling process. In practice, there is a range of possibilities between these two extremes that combine the skills and expertise of professionals with the local knowledge and enthusiasm of community members, both of which are likely to be important ingredients of a successful community profile.

If the profile is to be taken seriously, especially by those in positions of authority who are responsible for allocating resources, then it needs to be seen to be undertaken as systematically and professionally as resources will allow. However, this should not be an overriding consideration that stifles participants' creativity and spontaneity. As we are at pains to point out, community involvement is important to the process and it can also help to furnish the finished product with colour and an insight that outsiders may find more difficult to supply. Therefore there ideally needs to be a balance between the more objective, expert assistance provided by outside agencies and the enthusiastic insider understanding of the residents. One way to achieve this balance is through a working partnership of all stakeholders. Partnership working has become common practice as a way of planning and delivering services at local, district and regional levels, and these often involve local community members. You will need to decide on the balance of control within the partnership between representatives of the local community and non-resident stakeholders.

Means of involving stakeholders

Having discussed the level of control and ownership of the profiling process by the community in relation to other stakeholders, we now look at the different ways in which individuals might be involved. There are perhaps three levels of involvement although in practice the categories are blurred (see Figure 4.2).

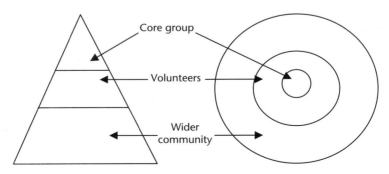

Figure 4.2   Levels of stakeholder involvement

The first level is that of the wider community where you can involve everyone even if it is to inform them about the profile and invite contributions and for them to take an active part in it. The second level is that of volunteers who want to help in a more practical way with the profile. You may wish also to develop a core group of individuals who will plan and manage the profiling process.

Involving the wider community

You can involve the wider community and all stakeholders in your community profile in two ways: first, by keeping everyone informed about each stage of the process and, second, through gathering information from as many members of the community as possible. Keeping the community informed about how the profile is progressing is important for a number of reasons. In the initial stages there may be considerable suspicion about the motives of those organizing the profile. Who are they? Where are they from? Why are they interested in us? It is important therefore to build understanding and trust through explaining clearly what the profile is for, how it will be undertaken and the timetable of events. Later in the process it may be necessary to inform the community about the preliminary findings, perhaps to check that no major mistakes or misrepresentations have been made. Finally, when the report has been completed, you can give the results back to the community in a form that is accessible and understandable, and involve them in action planning (see Chapter 9).

Many people undertaking community profiles prepare a press release or a leaflet before, during and possibly after the process. This basic publicity can be supplemented with conveniently placed, eye-catching posters and by ensuring that as many people as possible are talking – in an informed way – about the profile. Pubs, post offices, village halls and notice boards outside schools are all good places to start passing the word out about what is happening. You can also inform the community about the findings through developing a website, circulating emails and text messages, producing newsletters and putting on exhibitions and displays.

Another means of involving the wider community is by obtaining information and opinion directly from members of the community. Methods for obtaining primary data are explored in Chapter 7 and can include feedback systems on your website, although particular attention should be drawn to those methods that seek to involve as many residents as possible, such as surveys. There are several techniques you can use for maximizing participation in surveys such as running a free prize draw to encourage completion of questionnaires, inviting responses to initial findings through the inclusion of tear-off slips attached to newsletters or leaflets, and through organizing discussion groups around particular themes and issues. Figure 4.3 provides some hints on contacting groups in the community.

- It is often difficult to get people to come to public meetings. So, to begin with, work through established groups such as parent and toddler groups, elderly persons' lunch clubs, youth groups, etc.
- Use established channels of communication and networks
- Watch out for the pitfalls of utilizing existing groups, i.e. avoid cliques and involve everyone
- If there is little community organization currently in existence, then write into the planning process time and resources for community development

Figure 4.3 Working with existing groups or forming new groups

Involving volunteers

The next level at which stakeholders might be involved is that of providing practical assistance in the work of undertaking the profile. There is usually a pool of people within any community who would like to do something different or make better use of their skills or make a contribution to their community. Many just see it as a good opportunity to meet their neighbours and get to know more about their community. Offering people a practical task may be an effective way of involving them. The knowledge and skills required can range from computer work to making the tea and can include mapping, interviewing, word processing, drawing cartoons, designing layouts for reports and posters, chairing public meetings, leafleting and talking to the press. Figure 4.4 shows an example of how volunteers were used to assist with a community survey in Wales.

As part of its programme to research community needs and issues involved in the holistic regeneration of the Upper Dulais Valley, Cwmdulais Uchaf Communities First Partnership designed and implemented a community questionnaire.

It was decided that implementation be carried out by the Partnership and steering groups; everyone involved would hand-deliver a questionnaire to each house on their allotted streets. The method would be to door knock initially, to explain the questionnaire, and if no response the questionnaire be posted through. It was decided that two weeks [would] be ample time to complete the questionnaire and collection duly proceeded. Needless to say, results varied from street to street, volunteer to volunteer ... Individual response ranged from 10% to 90%, with the overall return closing at 52%.

Figure 4.4 Involving volunteers in a community survey: an example

Source: Cwmdulais Uchaf Communities First Partnership (2004) *The Community Profile: 7*

Many of these skills can be learned quickly and becoming involved in community profiling offers a good opportunity for people to acquire them if appropriate support is provided. Some groups of residents who have undertaken community profiles have themselves subsequently established community consultancy schemes (see Taylor *et al.* 2002). However, there may be people, perhaps retired, who already have such skills and knowledge. It is therefore valuable to recruit a pool of volunteers with a wide range of skills available that can be called on to provide assistance.

There are three further issues you will need to consider in developing a strategy for community involvement. The first is confidentiality. Members of the community may be unhappy about providing personal information to people they know, for example during interviews as part of a survey. This will need to be considered in making decisions about using members of the community to undertake interview work or analyse confidential interviews. (See Appendix 2 for further comments about the issue of confidentiality.)

The second issue is whether to pay volunteers for their work on the profile. If you have funds available, paying key people can be seen as a way of ensuring a consistent level of input, although there may be a danger that others who are not paid will refuse to become involved. Payment could be made per day or for discrete pieces of work such as a certain amount for each interview. Some profiles have offered volunteers a 'reward' for their help; others have even offered such 'rewards' to all interviewees.

The third issue relates to the balance between, on the one hand, training and supervising people in the community to undertake certain tasks and, on the other, paying a professional to do all or part of the work for you. While the first method will help to increase such skills within the community and will ensure a higher degree of community involvement in the process, it will also take longer and is likely to require considerable person power.

Further issues relating to local volunteers' role in the survey process, such as the best method of recruitment and a checklist for training interviewers, are discussed in more detail in Appendix 2.

Involving the core group

The community as a whole cannot manage the profile; a meeting of several hundred people would find it hard to make decisions. Also, not everyone who wants to be involved is happy in meetings or wishes to have a say in organizing the process. There is, however, a need for someone, or preferably a small group, to make the decisions, plan and organize the process, and make sure things happen on time. In profiles covering single issues or small areas the project may be managed by just one individual, but generally there will be a larger steering group of stakeholders involved. For some community profiles you may wish to consider both a smaller steering group that makes most of the decisions and a larger advisory body of stakeholders that meets less regularly but may have a broader range of expertise and knowledge.

How are these people to be recruited? In most cases they will be self-selected; perhaps they are the originators of the profile or have responded to invitations to join the steering group. However, when you are putting together a group, some attention should be paid to ensuring that all sections of the community are represented, and that as far as possible those people do represent others. For example, members from existing groups such as black and minority ethnic associations or area youth committees may wish to take part, or steering group members could be elected from different sectors of an estate. A steering group, especially when it becomes the management group, is the driving force behind the profile, and should provide others with motivation and enthusiasm. Involving the community in the group can go a long way towards helping that process.

Some community profiles may employ a full- or part-time project worker to take them forward. This person may have detailed knowledge of the community, with important local contacts. He or she can take on a variety of the profiling tasks described in this book, although the important ones will involve record keeping, coordinating the various activities, timekeeping and project managing, and supervising volunteers and other helpers. When a profile is initiated by a statutory organization such as a local authority department, a formal body such as an area-based regeneration agency, or even a voluntary organization, this role may be filled by someone from that agency or seconded from another organization. However this post is filled, it is important that the project worker's role is seen as a coordinating one that facilitates rather than frustrates community and stakeholder involvement. It is especially important that the project worker has clear lines of accountability.

When to involve stakeholders

Having considered the possible *levels* of stakeholder involvement we can now explore how people might get involved through all the *stages* of the community profiling process. We refer readers to the stages identified in Figure 3.1 in the previous chapter, which we now consider in turn.

Preparing the ground

Once the process of undertaking a community profile has become more than an idea, you will need to take steps to prepare the ground. As in all preparatory work, this stage will set the foundation on which the rest of the process rests, so it is important to get it right. In order to do so you need to involve stakeholders and the community, both to ensure their support and also to provide essential information.

A steering group of stakeholders needs to be set up as early as possible along the lines described in Chapter 3, involving members of the community, and ensuring that *all* sections of the community are in some way represented, if at all possible. In putting together members of the steering group, you need to consider the following issues. Will the community support the steering group? How will it be seen by the community? Are the members well respected?

The initial planning of the profile should involve the community in considerations of what are the boundaries of the community to be profiled and what defines the community. Initial contacts should be made with as many local groups and key stakeholders as possible, such as community activists and leaders, neighbourhood representatives and locally based professionals. Are they supportive of the idea to undertake a profile? What can they offer? Have they any further suggestions about the process that have not yet been considered? In identifying the resources that exist within the community that can be mobilized on behalf of the profile, it is important to include members of the community and other stakeholders who have relevant skills: market research, photography, computing, design and layout skills, and so on. Do groups, organizations or individuals have computers that can be used? Are there meeting places for both small and large meetings? Initial clarification of the aims and objectives need to be checked out with the community. What exactly is the purpose of the profile? Who owns it? Who is controlling it?

Once a steering group has been established, and some of the key stakeholders contacted, it is time to ensure that the wider community is approached. This is often undertaken through one or more public meetings in easily accessible and appropriate venues. Publicity for both the meetings and the profile itself can take a variety of forms, the most common being a website (either a dedicated one or through those belonging to other organizations), leaflets, posters and press releases (see Figure 4.5). Whatever form of publicity you choose, you should ensure that you address the following issues. Does your information tell people exactly what is happening, why, when, how, and who

---

To raise awareness of the profile, encourage involvement and trust, identify volunteers, clarify issues and sound out ideas etc.:

- Make use of the local press, TV and radio to publicize the project and also to keep people informed of progress throughout
- Develop and keep updated a website which invites feedback and comment on the evolving profiling process
- Go to where people meet – outside schools, pubs, post offices on pension days, shops and so on
- Hold fun events with exhibitions, refreshments and stalls in conjunction with stakeholders

---

Figure 4.5   Publicity

is doing it? Is it short, to the point and readable? Does it need to be in languages other than English? Can leaflets be put through everyone's door? How else could they be distributed?

Fieldwork and reporting

After the preparation comes the main part of the process: the fieldwork. This involves gathering all the information, from primary or secondary sources, putting it together and analysing it, then producing a draft profile. Much of the emphasis on involvement by the community in the preparatory stage was through the steering group. In this stage, volunteers can make a significant input to the work, although the steering group or management group will still be making some decisions and the wider community will be involved through supplying much of the information.

You can involve volunteers in all aspects of data collection, collation and analysis. Those who already have relevant skills will of course be invaluable, but the profile can offer a rare opportunity for other willing residents to acquire new skills and experience. What skills are required for your particular profile? Can they be taught? Are there people or organizations willing to pass on those skills?

Community and stakeholder involvement is crucial when you are drafting and **piloting** the questionnaire. It will ensure that the questionnaire addresses issues that have salience for members of the community to be profiled and in a way that has meaning for them. Is the language used and the way places and things are referred to locally relevant? Are the questions covered ones that residents will respond to, and enjoy answering? Also, when undertaking the fieldwork considerable thought must be given to methods of involving all the community. Many ethical and practical issues need to be considered when involving people who have disabilities, have literacy problems, are from a range of ethnic backgrounds and so on. Some suggestions for involving people who are more marginalized within communities can be found in Figure 4.6.

Techniques have been developed for assisting people with learning disabilities and people who have visual or hearing impairments, when undertaking tasks such as completing surveys. Specialist staff would assist you with these although the suggestions in Figure 4.7 may be considered.

Your draft profile can of course be altered later, but this may be the first output of the process and will give a significant impression of it. It is important, therefore, that you ensure that as far as possible it is clear and acceptable to the community and others it is aimed at. Community representatives may have a particular role to play in interpreting data, so it is worth seeking their views on the possible reasons for especially surprising findings. Are there any verbatim comments that can enliven the report? Ideally, a draft report needs to be discussed by stakeholders and especially the community that is its focus.

- Start to gather names from key people in places and networks which such groups are known to frequent, such as youth clubs, places of worship and day care centres
- Ask respondents if they know of people in similar situations or groups that you can interview – this method of obtaining more respondents is known as 'snowballing'
- As most people are likely to respond better to interviewers they see as more like themselves, it is often a good idea for a woman to interview women, young interviewers to interview young people, Asians to speak to Asians, etc.
- For some minority ethnic groups you will need to have interviewers who speak the minority language
- If you have more than one interviewer using the same language, they should meet together and agree on a consistent way of translating each question
- Where people may have a disability or behavioural problem, ask staff from residential or day care provision to assist, if this is acceptable to the respondent, or involve an advocate for the interviewee

Figure 4.6   Reaching the 'hard to reach' groups

- For people who are hard of hearing, lip-reading and writing down are recommended
- For deaf people who use British Sign Language (BSL), typetalk, a videophone or minicom can be used; many deaf non-BSL speakers rely on lip-reading or lip-speaking
- For blind and partially sighted people the use of tape recordings, increased size of font and use of a Word to Braille machine are all recommended
- Many people with learning difficulties prefer large print and symbols, and others prefer a combination of formats, such as audio tape and large print or audio tape and symbols
- Computer disks, email (to be accessed by specialist technology) and textphones are also of use

Figure 4.7   Suggestions for communication with people with disabilities

This can be achieved through a series of public meetings; on your website; by presenting key findings at a public exhibition and/or stakeholder workshops and inviting comments; by delivering a summary sheet with a slip for comments; or simply through feedback from stakeholders and the community representatives involved in the project. When you have made any further changes the final profile can be produced. As with the draft report, it is very important to ensure that everyone who contributed has a copy, or access to a copy, and that members of the wider community are aware that the profile has been produced.

Action planning

Once you have completed all the fieldwork and have produced the community profile, it is time to do something with it. What that is will largely depend on the original aims and objectives, but also on any changes that have been made to those in the course of the process, possibly as a result of the input by the community. Whatever uses the profile will be put to, it is likely to affect the community in some way, perhaps through campaigning for additional resources or changes in service provision, or merely to enlighten and raise the awareness of members of the community and decision makers about issues relevant to that community. As stakeholders and other members of the community are likely to be affected by the profile, it is essential that they have a further opportunity to become involved at this stage.

It is of course important that you involve stakeholders and the community in whatever event you use to launch the profile and in developments that occur as a result. You should also find further means to feed back to the community the findings of the profile. We explore further some of these uses and the potential for community involvement in Chapter 9.

Summary of key issues

In this chapter, we have explored issues facing those intending to undertake a profile when considering how best to encourage active involvement by the community and other stakeholders. Initially, you need to consider the ethical implications and values underlying the concept of participative research, especially the potential effects that professional assistance can have on the community. Like many services offered to a community, a community profile can serve to repress and control the community further, or it can become a powerful tool in assisting the process of empowerment and community capacity building.

Next, you need to have a clear understanding of the overall structure of the community that is the subject of the profile. What are the divisions, conflicts and power structures? What are the common bonds? Where are the boundaries? What are the bases for the social and cultural networks? With that understanding you can develop the aims and objectives of the profile and check them with stakeholders and the community.

You then need to understand and be aware of the methods and processes of undertaking the exercise. This extends from the initial planning stages through to the final production and its subsequent use and revisions. As well as involving relevant stakeholders, all sections of the defined community should be heard; and it is important for you not only to listen to what members of the community are saying, but also to enable them to participate in a meaningful way in the process itself.

Finally, therefore, issues of ownership and management of the whole process are important. If members of the community are in any way to control it, what mechanisms should there be? It is essential that you involve the widest possible section of the community, and from these members and other stakeholders draw on the resources of both a group of voluntary helpers and individuals who can form a partnership with the aim of steering the community profile. In turn, those volunteers or core group members must find ways of being accountable to the wider community. There must be adequate and sensitive support and training for those who need it and also sufficient time allocated for the profile to proceed at a pace that will maintain the maximum amount of community involvement.

References

Etzioni, A. (1996) *The New Golden Rule: Community and Morality in a Democratic Society*. New York: Basic Books.

Haggstrom, W.C. (1970) 'The psychological implications of the community development process', in L.J. Cary (ed.) *Community Development as a Process*. Columbia, MD: University of Missouri Press.

Hillery, G. (1955) 'Definitions of community: areas of agreement', *Rural Sociology*, 20: 111–22.

Stacey, M. (1969) 'The myth of community studies', *British Journal of Sociology*, 20(2): 34–47.

Taylor, M., Zahno, K., Thake, S., Nock, M. and Jarman, K. (2002) *Exploring the Field of Residents' Consultancy*, Research Report 382. London: Department for Education and Skills.

5   Selecting methods

Having established a group to oversee your community profile and agreed aims and objectives for your project you will now have to make decisions about which methods to use to collect the information that you need. This chapter takes you through the process of thinking about the kinds of methods to use to achieve different purposes and the level and type of resources that are necessary to implement these methods. We also provide an overview of the advantages and disadvantages of the different approaches and methods that are discussed in greater detail in Chapters 6 and 7. The stages in the process of deciding which methods to use that are discussed in this chapter are summarized in the 'decision tree' Figure 5.1 (opposite).

Matching method to purpose

Selecting the methods that you will use in your community profile entails consideration of the overall purpose and objectives of your profile, the questions that you are seeking to answer, possible sources of information and the methods that are most likely to elicit that information. In order to fulfil your overall purpose it is likely that there will be a number of different objectives that you would like your community profile to meet. However, make sure that you do not have too many objectives; if you do you risk making the project unwieldy and less likely to be completed successfully. If in your initial planning your list of objectives is very long, assign priorities to each objective and then focus on the top three or four.

Once your objectives are finalized you should go on to specify the questions that you need to ask to meet each objective and then to identify the most appropriate methods for answering those questions. (See Figure 5.2 for an example.) It is worth spending some time working up the research questions. The more precisely these are specified then the more likely it is that you will select methods that will generate appropriate and relevant information.

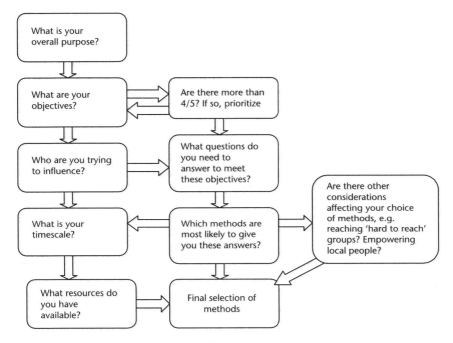

Figure 5.1   Selecting research methods: decision tree

In addition it may be important for your overall purpose to ensure that the way in which you collect the information conforms to certain other values that you feel are important, for example the need to involve as many members of the community as possible (see Chapter 4 for further details on involving the community). You will also need to make sure that you take account of ethical issues in selecting your methods. These will include ensuring that information that is provided to you is kept confidential, and making sure that people providing information to you do not feel pressurized in any way and freely give their consent to participating. For example, Packham (1998) argues that some research methods are exploitative and deskilling of their subjects and are therefore inappropriate to use in a community development context.

The final consideration is likely to be the timescale within which you want or need to complete the profile. Is there an externally imposed deadline that you are working towards, for example a deadline for funding proposals or a date for submissions to a consultation or a meeting at which you want your report to be considered? If so, you need to take this into account as well. Some methods, for example large, interview-based surveys, take much longer to set up and complete than others such as discussion groups.

The overriding aim that you need to keep in mind in selecting methods is

Objective	Research questions	Possible methods
To gain a better understanding of the needs of the local community	What is the structure (age, gender, ethnicity) of the local population?	Analysis of census data
	What do we know about the employment status of the adult population?	Analysis of census data
	What local services do people currently make use of?	Survey; discussion groups
	What do people think of local services?	Survey; discussion groups
To identify what services are currently available in the local community	What services currently exist and where are they located?	Walkabout/observation
	Who provides them?	Council and other agency directories of services
	Who makes use of local services? Are any groups excluded?	Interviews with service managers; discussion groups
To identify gaps in service provision	What additional services are needed by the local community?	Comparison of data on population with data from audit of services; survey; discussion groups

Figure 5.2   Objectives, research questions and methods: some examples

to obtain sufficient relevant, good quality information to answer the questions you have set yourselves without becoming embroiled in an over-complicated, lengthy and potentially costly exercise that saps stakeholders' enthusiasm and commitment.

Identifying resources

As part of the planning process (see Chapter 3) the group will have identified the resources that it has or has access to. This will be an important consideration in deciding on what methods to use. Some methods are considerably more resource-intensive than others. Before you can make a final decision on the methods, you will need to have a clear picture of which of the following resources you have available:

- existing information (see Chapter 6);
- people – with the time to undertake a range of different tasks;

- skills – in relation to survey or questionnaire design, interviewing, word processing, data inputting and analysis, publicity;
- equipment – computers, tape recorders, storage space, telephone, photocopier;
- money.

Of these resources the most important are probably people with the necessary time and skills available, and money. The kinds of skills that are relevant include: project management; questionnaire design; obtaining data; interviewing; inputting data; data analysis; report writing. The relationship between these types of resources is also critical. You may want to fill in the grid (Figure 5.3a) to decide which of these combinations best describes your group and then consider the implications as shown in Figure 5.3b.

There are other considerations in making decisions about the deployment of resources. First, even where you have considerable resources and could 'buy in' a professional researcher or consultant to undertake the process for you,

Type of resource	High availability (✓)	Low availability (✓)
People – time		
Skills/expertise		
Money		

Figure 5.3a Relationship between different types of resources

Time + skills + money	= Take your pick of appropriate methods
Time + skills	= Choose methods that are labour (not money) intensive e.g., making use of volunteers to undertake survey work
Time + money	= Buy in expertise but consider using volunteers trained and supervised by your expert
Time (low skills and money)	= Select very simple methods that can be carried out by volunteers; seek out free advice
Skills (low time and money)	= Make maximum use of existing data; consider supplementing this with some discussion groups
Money (low time and skills)	= Engage a consultant to do the work for you; seek out expertise in relation to commissioning
None of these resources	= Consider whether undertaking a community profile is the right thing to do at the current time; consider instead ways in which you might boost the resources available to your group.

Figure 5.3b Implications of different combinations of resources

there might nevertheless be strong reasons for not doing so, for doing it yourself. These reasons relate to the purpose of the community profiling exercise. If that purpose is, in part, to do with building up the skills, capacity and confidence of the local community then a 'do-it-yourself' approach might be preferable as it can make a significant contribution towards community development (see Chapter 4). On the other hand, if the overall purpose is to provide hard-hitting research evidence to support a local campaign then it might be the case that a professional researcher or consultant will be able to undertake work that is more persuasive to an external audience. However, even when this is the conclusion that you reach, your group will still need to be closely involved in specifying the project, commissioning the researcher or consultant and managing the process. (See Chapter 4 for a more detailed discussion of commissioning researchers.)

Doing the whole community profile yourself and commissioning an external researcher or consultant are at opposite ends of a spectrum with a number of points in between that might be worth considering. For example, you might want to commission an external researcher or consultant but specify that they have to employ local people as researchers or interviewers. A second possibility is to seek some (often free) expertise from a local college or university. For example, universities that offer degrees in Youth and Community Work often require students to undertake assessed research projects focusing on a particular neighbourhood. (See Packham 1998 for an example of an approach used at Manchester Metropolitan University.) Partnerships between colleges and universities can bring real benefits to both partners in terms of the quality of work undertaken and the development of longer-term links. However, for such partnerships to be fruitful there needs to be good communication between partners to ensure that both the community and the university each understands what the other wants to achieve through the project. Also, students undertaking community-based research will require institutional support and guidance from their tutor. Finally, you might want to consider using a resource pack or toolkit that allows you to use an 'off-the-shelf' resource that has been tested elsewhere, thus minimizing the resources needed to develop, for example, a questionnaire. (See the reference to Compass in Figure 8.11.)

Approaches

Having considered the questions you want to ask, the resources you have available and other issues that you need to take account of, you are now in a position to decide on which methods to use. There are two dimensions to this process. The first relates to the balance between the collection of new (primary) information and making use of existing (secondary) information; the

	Quantitative	**Qualitative**
Primary	Survey data	Focus group discussions; case stories; observations; photographs
Secondary	Census data; health, crime, housing, education statistics	Newspaper articles; photographs

Figure 5.4   Primary vs secondary data; quantitative vs qualitative

second to whether you want or need predominantly quantitative information or predominantly qualitative.

Secondary data

This is the term used to refer to data or information that already exists without you having to collect it yourself. Of course, you will still need to get hold of it, interpret and make sense of it. Sources of **secondary data** and how to obtain and make use of it are discussed more fully in Chapter 6. However, at this stage it is worth pointing out that no matter what your community there will be some information somewhere that is likely to be of interest or relevance to you. Obtaining such information can be a cheap method to use. It may also have a number of other advantages. For example, where data on your area is part of a national data set it can allow you to make comparisons between your area and elsewhere or to track changes over time. However, it should be remembered that, precisely because the data has been collected for a purpose that is not your own, it may not exactly answer the questions that you want it to. Furthermore, you will need to check the 'fit' between your population and that covered by the information that you are using. For example, the community for the purpose of your profile may be defined by the boundaries of a housing estate or perceptions of what constitutes the neighbourhood, whereas the data you are seeking to use is more likely to relate to a ward or local authority district.

Secondary data can be **quantitative** or **qualitative**. For example, the census will give you quantitative information about the population living in your area and agencies such as the housing department, police, education authority and Primary Care Trust all regularly collect data on, respectively, homelessness, crime, educational attainment and health. Such data is generally fairly readily available although, in most cases, it is reported in terms of wards or other administrative areas, not necessarily by the neighbourhood or community that you are interested in.

You may also be able to make use of qualitative information about your area. This may take the form of, for example, newspaper reports, photographs of local events or places, minutes and other records of local organizations.

Primary data

In most cases secondary data, while it may be useful, will not deliver the answers to all the questions posed by your community profile. This will mean that you will also need to collect new information that is more precisely geared to answering your own research questions. Again, bearing in mind the considerations discussed above, you may choose to employ quantitative methods, qualitative methods or a mixture of the two. A detailed discussion of methods can be found in Chapter 7. However, in this section we briefly summarize a wide range of methods to help you select which are most useful for your purposes. Figure 5.5 summarizes the methods most commonly used in community profiling and briefly indicates what they are useful for and what the disadvantages are.

Quantitative approaches to the collection of **primary data** are predominantly concerned with collecting relatively straightforward information from relatively large numbers of people in answer to such questions as: How many? How often? What kind? The most common quantitative method used in community profiles is the social survey, which uses questions in a standard format as a means of collecting information from local people. Surveys can be administered by post, telephone, electronically or face to face. **Observations** can also yield quantitative information, for example the numbers of children using a playground or other local service at particular times of day.

Qualitative approaches are less concerned with issues that are amenable to quantification. Rather they are intended to provide answers to questions about what a smaller number of people think or feel about things, their perceptions, attitudes and experiences. Examples include: **semi-structured interviews** or unstructured interviews with a small number of people; focus group discussions; and case stories (see Figure 5.6).

Combining methods

Because different methods bring with them both advantages and disadvantages it is often worthwhile combining methods: quantitative and qualitative; primary and secondary data collection. This can result in the collection of richer information and a more comprehensive and rounded view of the community. In Figures 5.7 and 5.8 (p. 62) you can find two examples where data collection methods have been combined to good effect, in the assessment of a community's health needs in the first case, and in a wide-ranging community audit and needs study in the second. In Figure 5.9 (p. 63) a number of

Method	Useful for ...	Advantages	Disadvantages
Social survey	Obtaining extensive, quantifiable data from a large number of people	Can be both explanatory and descriptive; if properly carried out results are reliable	Designing a survey questionnaire and deciding on a sample require some technical skills
Telephone		Relatively quick and cheap to undertake	Not everyone has a telephone; issues around people who don't have English as a first language; predominantly closed questions, i.e. researcher sets the agenda
Postal		Relatively quick and cheap to undertake; can cover large numbers of people	Likely to generate a low response rate; may create difficulties for people with low level of literacy; predominantly closed questions, i.e. researcher sets the agenda
Face to face		Overcomes problems associated with poor literacy	Resource-intensive in terms of people's time; may need to include interpretation for people for whom English is not their first language; possibility of interviewer bias
Observation			
Community walkabout	Getting a feel for the physical aspects of a community; identifying location of services, community buildings etc.	Can generate useful information that could form the basis of a local directory	Can be time-consuming if done systematically

Figure 5.5 Continued

Method	Useful for ...	Advantages	Disadvantages
Participant observation	Describing aspects of the life of the community	Describes people's behaviour in a 'natural' setting, i.e. not in an artificial research setting such as an interview	Time-consuming and expensive; heavily dependent on the skills of the researcher
Case stories	Obtaining an in-depth account of an individual or group	Can provide illustrative material to add depth and richness to e.g. survey data	Issues about confidentiality and anonymity; not usually generalizable
Unstructured data collection	Scoping work; exploring issues in depth		
In-depth interviews	Obtaining in-depth information from a smaller number of people	Need to be undertaken by a skilled interviewer	Possibility of interviewer bias; data can be difficult to analyse; need to address issues of confidentiality
Focus groups	In-depth discussion of key issues and identification of options and priorities	Need to be conducted by a skilled facilitator	Data can be difficult to analyse
Secondary data			
Census and other national data	Tracking changes over time; providing a sampling frame	Difficult to guarantee attendance	May not be available for the precise boundaries that you are interested in; statistics presented in a standard way
Local statistics	Getting quantitative information on the local area from a reputable source	Cheap, readily available and comprehensive	May not be available for the precise boundaries that you are interested in; statistics presented in a standard way; involves approaching a number of different organizations

Method	Useful for ...	Advantages	Disadvantages
Service user data	Understanding the views of users of a specific service	Cheap and generally readily available; often easy to obtain – agencies delivering services often have systems in place, e.g. annual customer satisfaction surveys	Data is collected from a small, often self-selecting group of service users; no information is provided about those who do not use a service
Documentary analysis, e.g. minutes of local organizations, newspaper reports	Background and contextual information	Can provide insight into the concerns and issues affecting a neighbourhood over time	No way of knowing how accurate the records are or whether they present a very partial account

Figure 5.5   Advantages and disadvantages of different methods

Choose a questionnaire when:
- large numbers are involved
- 'facts' rather than opinions are sought
- data in a standard format is required
- wide geographic coverage is required
- time for the respondent to reflect could be useful
- long lists of statements need to be read
- researcher time is at a premium

Choose an interview when:
- smaller numbers are involved
- the enquiry is exploratory
- attitudes are sought
- complicated reasons for actions are sought
- sensitive areas are being explored
- complex situations exist
- non-verbal responses could be significant
- flexibility is required

Figure 5.6   Surveys: questionnaire or interview?

Source: Fuller, R. and Petch, A. (1995) *Practitioner Research: The Reflexive Social Worker.* Buckingham: Open University Press: 56.

The objective of this project was to explore the use of four methods to define health needs in a community with a view to formulating guidelines for practice-based assessment of health needs.

Four complementary methods of data collection were used for a specific neighbourhood consisting of 670 homes on an estate in Edinburgh. The methods used were: rapid participatory appraisal, postal survey, analysis of routinely available small areas statistics and the collation of practice-held information. Each method used gave insights into both health and healthcare needs, leading the researchers to conclude that 'a mix of assessment methods may provide more information about health needs than one method alone'.

Figure 5.7   Assessing health needs using a variety of methods

Source: Murray, S.A. and Graham, L.J.C. (1995) 'Practice-based health needs assessment: use of four methods in a small neighbourhood', *BMJ*, 310: 1443–8

The purpose of this study was to increase understanding of local needs in Blackpool and to undertake an audit of council services which contribute to the alleviation of social exclusion, poverty and disadvantage.

The study comprised the following main components:

• an audit of council services carried out by means of individual interviews with senior managers and an examination of all relevant strategic and service delivery documents

• a postal survey of existing community groups and voluntary organizations to identify those agencies providing services in the six wards on which the study was focused

• a community forum to inform the groups mailed as to the purpose of the study

• an interview survey of 600 residents in the six target wards

• community focus groups organized around structured questions

Figure 5.8   A multi-method community audit and needs study

Source: Barnsley, K. (1998) *Blackpool Community Audit*. Blackpool Borough Council

less commonly used methods that might be useful to your community profiling exercise are summarized. Again the importance of combining methods to achieve your overall purpose is emphasized.

'Hard to reach' groups

Many communities contain within them certain groups that are considered to be 'hard to reach' in terms of research or consultation exercises. Although they

- *Activity chart:* plotting people's activities each day or week; useful for understanding divisions of labour, roles and responsibilities in a community
- *Building survey:* recording the state of repair of buildings
- *External relationship profiling:* examining the role and impact of external organizations
- *Gender workshop:* separate sessions for women (or sometimes men) to analyse their situation, needs and priorities
- *Historical profile:* identifying and listing key events, beliefs and trends in a community's past and their importance for the present
- *Household livelihood analysis:* comparing sources of income and support with expenditure patterns and looking at coping strategies for times of hardship
- *Informal walk:* walking in a group without a definite route, stopping to chat and discuss issues as they arise
- *Mapping:* making maps showing various characteristics, e.g. resources
- *Organization review:* review of existing groups and organizations to assess their roles, membership, plans and potential
- *Personal history:* recording detailed oral accounts of individuals' lives, perhaps asking them to emphasize specific issues
- *Problem tree:* analysing the interrelationships among community issues and problems using a graphic based on a tree
- *Role play:* adopting the role of others and acting out scenarios
- *Seasonal calendar:* exploring changes taking place throughout the year, e.g. in work patterns or production
- *Semi-structured interview:* conversational open discussion using a checklist of questions as a flexible guide instead of a formal questionnaire; different types include individual, group, focus group and key informant
- *Simulation:* acting out a real event or activity in order to understand its effect
- *Skills survey:* assessing skills and talent in a community
- *Transect walk:* systematic walk through an area to observe and record key features, for instance land use zones

Figure 5.9 Possible methods of use to community profiling

Source: Wates, N. (2000) *The Community Planning Handbook.* London: Earthscan

are hard to reach they are, nevertheless, important if you are going to get a full picture of the community. Examples of groups that are traditionally 'hard to reach' include:

- white working-class men;
- Asian women;

- children and young people;
- refugees and asylum seekers;
- Gypsies and travellers;
- homeless people;
- people with learning difficulties.

They are hard to reach for a variety of different reasons, including: not having English as a first language; poor levels of literacy; cultural reasons; reasons to do with their situation; not having an organization that provides a 'way in' to the group in question. Engaging with hard to reach groups is discussed in more detail in Chapters 4 and 6; however, in the context of the discussion of selecting research methods it is important to consider whether your choice of methods will, in effect, exclude certain groups and, if so, how you will overcome this to ensure that you achieve a full picture of your community and its residents. Knowing how the local population is made up is an important first step in ensuring that you choose methods that are appropriate. The census of population will give you this basic information about the make-up of the population in your area (see Chapter 6). (For an example of an interesting approach to obtaining children's views of their neighbourhood see Figure 5.10.)

This Canadian project wanted to learn from children about their use of, and needs in, neighbourhood spaces. Using a technique called cognitive mapping children were able to map places that were important to them. In particular the researchers were able to gain an insight into children's perceptions of features of the urban landscape, notably paths, edges, districts, nodes and landmarks.

Figure 5.10   Obtaining children's views of their neighbourhood

Source: Halseth, G. and Doddridge, J. (2000) 'Children's cognitive mapping: a potential tool for neigh-bourhood planning', *Environment and Planning B: Planning and Design*, 27: 565–82

Summary of key issues

This chapter has built on the earlier chapter on planning by considering the factors that need to be taken into account in deciding on the methods to be used for your community profile. Key issues include: the importance of matching method to purpose; developing research questions and then considering what is the best method to use to answer them; taking account of the resources available and using them to best effect; and striking a balance between the use and collection of primary and secondary data on the one hand and quantitative and qualitative methods on the other. In the next two chapters we discuss in more detail how you go about collecting and using secondary information and primary information.

Reference

Packham, C. (1998) 'Community auditing as community development', *Community Development Journal*, 3(3): 249–59.

6 Making use of existing information

Collecting, collating and analysing new data is both time-consuming and resource-intensive. So before investing precious resources in collecting new information it is important to check what data is already available that might be of use and relevance to your community profile. Whatever the community that you are profiling there is almost certainly some existing – or secondary – data that will be helpful to you. A thorough search for, and judicious use of, this information could save you both time and money. Since writing the first edition of this book the internet has developed and this, together with the electronic publication of all kinds of data and information, means that it is now possible to track down a wide range of information, often in accessible and easy-to-use formats.

This chapter is intended to guide you through the process of thinking about what kinds of existing or secondary information might be useful to you, tracking it down and making use of it as part of your profile.

How can secondary information contribute to your profile?

In the introduction above, we have suggested that using secondary information can save you time and money; why collect data if someone else has already done the job for you? (However, in the section on making use of existing data (pages 72–74) we discuss the need for a degree of caution.) But this is not the only reason for using the data and information that is already around.

If you are intending to undertake a survey in your local community, secondary data can help you to understand the composition of the population in your local area and to make sure that your sample is representative or, in other words, that the composition of the sample that you survey looks pretty much the same as the population as a whole. (For further information on sampling see Appendix 2.)

A second reason for using secondary information is to provide a context for, or comparison with, the information that you collect through your profile. For example, you might collect information for your community on health and ill health. However, without some basis for comparison you will not be able to tell whether these findings are generally good or whether they indicate that some action is needed. In this case you will need to compare your findings on health and health status to those for the wider area or for other people in the area with a similar age, gender or ethnic profile. Using existing sources of data you can compare your locality with others in the local area, in the region or nationally.

Another benefit of using existing sources of data is that you can often track trends over time. This allows you to develop a view as to whether things in your area are generally getting better or worse.

Finally, you will not be able to collect data – especially quantitative data – on all the topics that you might be interested in. For example, it is very difficult for a community organization to collect reliable information on morbidity and mortality (illness and death); it is generally better to rely instead on official statistics from the Primary Care Trust and then add to this with locally collected information on attitudes to health, access to services and so on.

Types of secondary information

Once you start looking for information about your local area you risk becoming the victim of 'information overload'. There is a huge amount of potentially useful information available from a number of different sources. In considering whether or not it is useful for your purposes you need to address the questions not only about the credibility and **reliability** of the data, as indicated towards the end of the chapter, but also its relevance to your purposes. Return to the research questions that you identified for your community profile (see Chapter 5) and consider which of these could, potentially, be answered through secondary data and then look for information around these topics. Alternatively you might first want to undertake an exploratory trawl to see 'what's out there' (see Figure 6.1, overleaf, for some ideas of types of secondary information). The internet is an indispensable tool for this purpose; if you do not yourselves have access to the internet then you will be able to do so through your local library. The librarian should also be able to guide you to appropriate websites about the local area. Many local authorities provide a wide range of local information online and this can be a very useful starting point to find out what's easily available. (See Figure 6.2, overleaf, for an example of the kinds of information that local authorities make available.)

Websites: there are many websites that might be of use but make sure that you are only using information from credible sources (see Appendix 3 for a summary of the main sites and go to www.vts.intute.ac.uk/tutorial/social-research-methods for a free tutorial on using the internet for social research

Local newspapers: to give an idea of what the local concerns and issues are

Publicly available records: for example, minutes of meetings of local organizations

Official reports and statistics: this is the main source of secondary data and will generally be reputable; however, even official reports and statistics should be used critically and with a degree of caution (see Figure 6.4)

Figure 6.1 Types of secondary information

Census 2001: key statistics from the 2001 census and comparisons with 1991

Geographical areas: district areas, population densities

Population: estimates and projections

Other demographic trends: migration, births and deaths

Unemployment: totals, percentages, youth, long term

Agriculture: labour force, distribution of holdings, estimated standard output

Other economic trends: business, employment, employment land, RPI, GDP

Housing: prices, council tax bands, completions, land availability, forecasts etc.

Tourism: number of visitors, tourist spending, weather characteristics

Education and training: school types, pupil:teacher numbers, class sizes, training statistics

Social trends: benefits information, lone parents, lone pensioners, long-term illness

Transportation: car ownership, aircraft movements

Environment: conservation areas, waste disposal, water distribution

Health: birth rates, mortality rates

Community safety: road accidents, crime, fire and rescue, trading standards

Externally funded programmes: European and UK funding

Deprivation indices: index of multiple deprivation, census indicators

Community appraisals: community appraisal reports

Performance indicators: dealing with the public, service provision

Electoral statistics: number of electors, election results

Figure 6.2 Example of information available online from Devon County Council

Source: www.devon.gov.uk/dris/main_mnu.html, accessed 9 November 2006

The local context

As part of the preliminary work for your community profile you may want to scope out the kinds of issues that might be relevant by looking at back copies of the local paper; these can highlight the kinds of issues that have been of concern in recent months. In addition agendas and minutes of local organizations can provide an insight into what is going on in the area.

You can also get a general feel for the kind of community that this is by going to websites such as www.upmystreet.com, which provide some basic information about specific areas and also a 'profile' of the local community developed by analysing the local population and then comparing it to areas that have similar populations. (See Figure 6.3, overleaf, for a profile of a part of Leeds taken from upmystreet.com.)

About the population

Whatever the ultimate purpose of your community profile you will almost certainly need information about the population in your area. How many people live in the area? How old are they? What proportion of the population are under 5 or over 75? What ethnic groups does the population belong to? How many people have a disability? What kinds of households do people live in? And so on. The main source of information about population in any area in the UK is the census of population. This takes place every ten years and, in principle, asks all adults a number of questions about themselves, their households, their employment and other characteristics. All residents are required by law to complete the census questionnaire. As a result it is the most comprehensive source of population information and is used by a wide range of government departments and other local and regional public agencies for planning services and allocating resources. The most recent census took place in April 2001 and the next one is planned for 2011.

Following the 2001 census, results have been freely available online from www.statistics.gov.uk/census/ (with similar sites for Scotland and Northern Ireland). In addition local councils often publish their own neighbourhood profiles based on census data. Census data can be obtained online in the form of either maps or tables. The results are available for different areas including: local government areas; health authority areas; Parliamentary constituencies; parishes; and postcode areas. Census data is also available for smaller areas known as **output areas** (which, in 2001, replaced enumeration districts). Each output area contains around 125 households. The output areas then 'nest' within wards and parishes. Output areas have also been grouped to form **super output areas** (SOAs), which are widely used to present key data from the census. In addition to census data the Office for National Statistics also publishes annual estimates of the population for district level and above.

Often, many of the people who live in this sort of postcode will be suburban privately renting professionals. These are known as type 19 in the ACORN classification and 1.09% of the UK's population live in this type.

Neighbourhoods fitting this profile are found in Richmond-upon-Thames, Sutton and Bromley in Outer London, and in Cheltenham, St Albans and Guildford. Here is an overview of the likely preferences and features of your neighbourhood:

Family income	High
Interest in current affairs	Very high
Housing with mortgage	Medium
Educated to degree	Very high
Couples with children	Very low
Have satellite TV	Very low

These young people have made a lifestyle choice to reside close enough to the major conurbations to obtain the benefits of the city without actually living in its centre. In their twenties and early thirties, they are well educated and are developing their careers in professional and managerial jobs.

They are living in purpose-built flats in attractive suburbs and satellite towns. Many are still renting, although some have purchased their homes.

They use diverse means to get around. Where possible they will travel to work by public transport, by bike or on foot. However, the majority do have a car and will often buy new, expensive models.

These people are very comfortable using the internet in all aspects of their life including financial services, purchasing gifts, CDs and books, and booking their holidays and leisure activities online.

For holidays, the USA, Canada and other long-haul destinations are popular, as are weekend breaks and winter snow holidays. In their spare time they enjoy sport and exercise. They also like spending their money on shopping for clothes and eating out.

They are interested in current affairs, and whilst they tend to read mainly the broadsheet papers, they show no bias to any particular title.

Figure 6.3   Profile of Headingley in Leeds, taken from upmystreet.com

About specific issues

In addition to general information about the composition and characteristics of the population you may want information about more specific issues. A good place to start is the government's neighbourhood statistics website (www.neighbourhood.statistics.gov.uk). This provides a wide range of small area statistics covering the following topics:

- 2001 census;
- access to services;
- community well-being/social environment;
- crime and community safety;
- economic deprivation;
- education, skills and training;
- health and social care;
- housing;
- indicators;
- English Indices of Deprivation;
- people and environment;
- work deprivation.

In addition you can obtain data for your local area (sometimes at the level of local authority district and sometimes at ward level) on all of the following topics:

- Deprivation: the Index of Multiple Deprivation ranks all local authority districts and wards in England in terms of a composite indicator of deprivation.
- Benefits and pensions: the Department for Work and Pensions provides data sets relating to numbers of people in localities in receipt of all the major pensions and benefits.
- Education: the Department for Education and Skills publishes attainment levels for local authority areas and for specific schools at Key Stages 1 and 2, GCSE and A level. In addition data is available on post-16 education for each area. This data can be obtained nationally through the DfES website and should also be available locally from the Local Education Authority.
- Crime: the Home Office publishes data on notifiable offences recorded by the police at Crime and Disorder Reduction Partnership level up to national level. Again this is available nationally from the Home Office and locally through the local Crime and Disorder Reduction Partnership.
- Health: the Director of Public Health publishes an annual public health report for the area.
- Housing: some information on housing, e.g. forms of tenure and types of housing, can be obtained from the census. In addition the local authority's housing department will be available to provide data on such things as the total housing stock, numbers of vacant housing and homelessness.
- Income and earnings: data is derived from the Annual Survey of Hours and Earnings.

- Employment: the Labour Force Survey is carried out annually and generates a huge amount of data on all aspects of employment.

About local services

Information about local statutory services can be obtained from a variety of different sources. It is worth checking to see if your local authority has compiled a Directory of Local Services which might serve as a useful basis for an audit of current provision. In addition you can check on the performance of key local services including those provided by the council by looking at the Audit Commission's report on your authority and the services it provides. Other agencies that inspect local services can also be useful sources of information on schools, nurseries and other provision for children (Ofsted inspection reports), social care (Social Services Inspectorate reports). In addition all local authorities have to undertake periodic customer satisfaction surveys and you should be able to access the findings from these. The Audit Commission's Area Profiles project brings together a wide range of local data to provide a profile of each local authority in England. It includes demographic information together with data on the performance of services, assessments made by independent inspectorates and residents' views as indicated by local surveys.

Making use of secondary data

While secondary data can be immensely helpful, fulfilling the kinds of functions outlined above, there are also potential pitfalls that you should be aware of. These generally arise from the fact that secondary data has not been collected with you or your community in mind; you will have to interpret and adapt this data to meet your own needs. In so doing you should consider the following key points (also summarized in Figure 6.4).

Where does the data come from?

First, consider where the data has come from. Is it from an organization that is credible and is likely to produce authoritative data that stands up to close scrutiny? Most of the data sources referred to in this chapter are 'official' sources – in other words, the data has been collected in a standardized way by local or national public agencies. This doesn't mean that there aren't sometimes disputes about the nature of official data. For example, there are frequent questions asked about the basis for measuring things like unemployment and hospital waiting lists that are often politically sensitive, and accusations have been made that the basis for collecting such information is changed so that it presents the government in a more positive light. However, in general, official

- *Who says so?* Where has the data come from? Is it a credible and authoritative source?
- *How do they know?* What methods have been used to collect the data? Do they seem sensible? If a sample is used does it seem big enough to say anything about the wider community?
- *Does the data measure what it's supposed to?* For example, do crime figures measure the actual numbers of offences committed or only those that are reported to the police?
- *Is it up to date?* Has the data been collected fairly recently?
- *Does it cover the right area?* How good a fit is there between the area that the data relates to and your area?
- *What doesn't the data tell you?* Is there anything that you need to know about this data to make it useable and relevant? If there is, can you find out the answer?

Figure 6.4   Questions to ask about secondary data

data – whether collected locally or nationally – has to conform to extremely high standards and is the most reliable that there is available.

Is the data valid?

A second question to ask is whether the data measures what it purports to measure. For example, official unemployment figures actually refer to the numbers of people who are not only out of work but also claiming benefit. Unemployed people who are not eligible for benefit are not included in the count and, conversely, some unemployed people who are not actually looking for work are included.

Related to this is the issue of samples and sample sizes. If the data that you are considering is derived from a survey and you find out that the number of people who answered the survey questions was small and all were friends of the person carrying out the research you would be entitled to question whether or not the data tells you anything useful about the wider population. Furthermore, if you then discover that the survey questionnaire was full of leading questions that would inevitably generate a particular kind of response then you should discard this data as being too biased to be useful. In other words you need to be confident that the data you are using has been collected using appropriate and rigorous methods.

Another way of thinking about this is to ask the following question. If someone else conducted the same piece of research or data gathering would the results be the same? If the data has been collected carefully using robust methods then the answer to this question should be 'yes'. However, if the data collection has been poorly designed and executed then the answer will probably be no.

Finally, consider whether or not the data is broadly in line with what you would expect to find. If not then it is worth thinking through possible explanations for this. For example, if a survey purports to show that the majority of the local population is in favour of extended opening hours for local pubs and you know that this has been an issue that has generated considerable controversy in the community in the past then it may be worth looking more closely at the data and the methods used to collect it. For example, is the sample used for the survey representative of the whole population? If it contains a disproportionate number of young men aged 17 to 25 then you might not be so surprised at this finding. Furthermore, if the survey was conducted outside the local pub at 11.00 p.m. on a Friday night then you would be even less surprised.

How up-to-date is the information?

Communities can change quite rapidly and so it is important to ensure that the data you are using is as up to date as possible. (This is one difficulty with the census, which is conducted only every ten years. The last one was in 2001 and so by the midway point between censuses the data is beginning to get out of date.) When you are looking at a data set always check that the figures are the most recent ones available.

What geographical area does the data cover?

One important difficulty that you are likely to face when using secondary data in the context of a community profile is that the administrative areas – wards, local authority districts, Primary Care Trust areas, police divisions – that are typically used as the basis for the collection of official data may not have the same boundaries as those which delineate your community or neighbourhood. Communities, especially those that are defined by local people themselves, do not necessarily fit administrative boundaries and, indeed, these may vary across agencies. So, if you are comparing data that you have collected with data from another source make sure that you are comparing 'like with like' in terms of the area covered.

Summary of key issues

Before embarking on a costly and resource-intensive exercise of collecting new data it is worth looking at existing data sources to check to what extent they can provide answers to at least some of the questions that you are addressing through your community profile. In addition secondary data can provide a basis for comparison with other areas as well as an understanding of the

Website	Information available	Comments
www.upmystreet.com	Type in your postcode to get information about the local area including: schools; local services; policing and crime rates; neighbourhood profiles can also be obtained based on the ACORN classification	The data is not always complete and the neighbourhood profiles are generated by analysing the composition of the population and then presenting a profile based on analysis of other neighbourhoods with similar populations
www.ofsted.gov.uk	You can download inspection reports for any local school, nursery or out of school club	Inspections are carried out within a prescribed inspection framework; as a result some aspects of local services are not mentioned
www.neighbourhood. statistics.gov.uk	Type in your postcode to download neighbourhood profiles produced by the Office for National Statistics; data available includes: the population, access to services, community well-being, crime and community safety, economic deprivation, education, skills and training, and housing	An authoritative source of data available at a number of different levels – ward, local authority area, super output area, health authority, education authority, parish
www.area.profiles.audit-commission.gov.uk	This website provides guidance on how to put together an area profile and also allows you to download a collection of performance indicators under ten quality of life themes	The geographical area used for area profiles are local authority areas; however, this website provides useful contextual data including access to statutory surveys such as the views of residents on local public services
www.statistics.gov.uk/census2001/	This site provides free access to data from the 2001 census on England; similar sites are also available for Scotland and Wales	Authoritative statistical data on all aspects of the population and its characteristics

Figure 6.5   Continued

Website	Information available	Comments
www.communities. gov.uk/index.asp?id=11 28444	The (English) Index of Multiple Deprivation 2004 is the most recent comprehensive measure of multiple deprivation; compares localities and ranks them according to the extent and intensity of deprivation	Composite index made up of indicators in relation to seven domains of deprivation
www.dwp.gov. uk/asd/statistics.asp	The Department for Work and Pensions publishes data sets which relate to different geographical areas on pensions and benefits, including: state pension; pension credit; income support; jobseekers allowance; attendance allowance; incapacity benefits	Useful but complex data sets
www.dfes.gov.uk/inyour area/	Type in the name of your local area or postcode to obtain statistics relating to schools and educational achievement pre- and post-16, by local authority area or ward	
www.crimestatistics. org.uk/output/ page1.asp	Type in your postcode to get the most up-to-date information on crime in your local authority area	
www.nomisweb.co.uk/	Provides statistics on the local labour market from a variety of different sources including the Annual Population Survey, Labour Force Survey, jobseekers allowance claimant count, DWP benefits, Annual Business Inquiry and the Annual Survey of Hours and Earnings	

Website	Information available	Comments
www.audit-commission.gov.uk/reports/NATIONAL-REPORT.asp?CategoryID=&ProdID=0D488A03-8C16-46fb-A454-7936FB5D5589	Provides information on the 45 quality of life indicators developed by the Audit Commission to show how a local area is performing economically, environmentally and socially	Provides a wide range of data at the local authority level; because data on the same indicators is collected for all local areas it is possible to make comparisons; the indicators could be used as the basis for comparisons between a local community and the local authority areas as a whole
All websites accessed 7 November 2006		

Figure 6.5   Annotated online sources of data

composition of the local population for the purposes of accurate sampling. The development of the internet has led to much easier access to a wide range of data sources of relevance to communities and neighbourhoods. This chapter has given an indication of some key data sources available either nationally or locally. When considering making use of secondary data in your community profile you need to ask some key questions. Where does the data come from and is this a credible and authoritative source? Is the data **valid** and does it measure what it purports to measure? Is the data up to date and to what geographical areas does it pertain?

References

Figure 6.5 provides an annotated list of online sources of information.

7 Collecting new information

Chapter 5 will have helped you decide the kinds of methods that are best for your group and the community profile you wish to undertake. Profiles can be compiled on the basis of data collected from the kind of secondary sources described in the previous chapter, but it is likely that in most cases you will not be able to get all the information you need from existing sources and that you will decide to collect new or primary data. In this chapter we will look in more detail at the main techniques used in the process of collecting primary data, the strengths and weaknesses of those techniques and at the issues involved in deciding which method is best suited to your particular community profile.

This chapter will look at three main techniques of collecting primary data of relevance to community profiling. These are *surveys*, *observation* and *in-depth data collection*. Surveys are one of the most common methods used for collecting information from a large number of people. There are two principal ways of conducting a survey: either respondents complete a questionnaire themselves or an interviewer asks the questions and records the answers. Further information of relevance to conducting surveys is set out in Appendix 2. Observing community activity and systematically recording those observations can also be used as a means of gathering information, and can add considerable interest and colour to the profile. Finally, we will consider some means of collecting in-depth information from individuals and groups.

Choosing a method

Whichever method you decide to use for collecting new information, there are three primary considerations; these are to be:

- specific;
- systematic;
- objective.

You need to be clear about what information you need, and clear about how you ask for it; muddled thinking can lead to muddled results. It is also essential that you collect information as carefully as possible. Failure to do so can invalidate the information collected and can discredit the whole profile in the eyes of those who are to make use of it, or be persuaded by the results. In the same way, it is vital that the views and opinions of those collecting the data do not interfere with the process. This must be kept in mind, especially when designing any questionnaire, asking questions, facilitating discussions, or interpreting what is being observed.

In deciding which techniques to use to collect new information, you will need to consider the issues listed in Figure 7.1. So, for example, if the community profile is mainly intended to be part of a broader community development exercise, it may be the case that the process is as important as the information collected, which might suggest the need for survey methods which maximize the opportunities for community participation, for example door-to-door interviewing. If, on the other hand, the aim is to persuade an organization that the community has significant needs which are currently not being met, then methods which result in lots of 'hard' statistical information may be more appropriate, such as a postal survey of a large sample.

- The purpose of the profile
- The aims and objectives of the project
- The type of information you want to collect – quantitative or qualitative, 'facts' or perceptions
- Who you want to obtain information from – individual residents, groups of residents, frontline service providers, community representatives
- The resources you have at your disposal – money, time, people
- The skills that you have within your group – questionnaire design, interviewing skills, computing expertise, data analysis, group work

---

Figure 7.1   Issues to consider when deciding on collecting new information

Surveys

In essence, a survey is a means of collecting information in a standard format from a relatively large number of people. Collecting information in a structured way is necessary if you want to be able to analyse that information relatively easily and also if you want to be able to compare the responses of different groups of people. However, information from surveys is only as good as the tools that are used to collect that information. This is an area where it is very easy to make mistakes that can invalidate almost all of the information collected. Given that surveys are costly to undertake in terms of both money and people resources, you should be quite sure that you really need to do a survey to collect the information you require.

Surveys can be divided into those which require respondents (those persons answering the questions) to complete the survey questionnaire themselves (self-completion questionnaires) and those which require that someone else asks the questions and records the responses (interview surveys).

Self-completion surveys

Self-completion surveys are usually posted or delivered to people's homes although increasing use is also being made of online or internet-based surveys. Postal surveys, in particular, can be relatively quick and easy to administer and it is possible to reach quite a lot of people in this way. The types of situation in which self-completion questionnaires might be useful are where you want to get a fairly superficial, broad-brush indication of issues from a relatively large group of people. In small communities, especially where those communities are geographically concentrated, they may be less useful. A short self-completion questionnaire may sometimes be appropriate for use in a group setting, for example in a classroom or as a short exercise as part of a community organization or faith group meeting.

Internet surveys are becoming increasingly popular. They can be faster, cheaper and easier to conduct than postal, telephone or door-to-door surveys. A questionnaire can either be sent by email or people can be encouraged to complete it on a website. Internet surveys are well suited for larger surveys and for some target populations (such as young males) that are difficult to reach by traditional survey methods. However, although surveys incur virtually no **coding** or data-entry costs because the data is captured electronically, there are issues in using this method including the high resource cost in terms of the time and skill needed to design and program the survey, the need to have email addresses for your sample, and the fact that not everyone has access to a computer linked to the internet. An internet survey could, however, be considered as part of a mixed-method approach (discussed more fully later in this chapter). For example, a local library could provide access to an online version of your questionnaire and library users invited to complete it using library computers.

More generally there are three main problems with self-completion questionnaires. The first is that people have to be reasonably literate in the language the questionnaire is written in to complete it. A second difficulty is that self-completion questionnaires work best with a relatively small number of 'tick box' questions. This may be problematic if you want to ask more 'open' questions or want respondents to give a more considered response. The third disadvantage is that they tend to result in quite low **response rates**. In other words, the proportion of those receiving a questionnaire who complete and return it may be low. In addition, your **response sample** (those completing and returning the questionnaire) may not be representative, as certain groups of people are notoriously reluctant to fill in questionnaires of this kind. Furthermore, a low response rate can also introduce a bias that distorts your results as it is often those who are most vulnerable, disadvantaged or alienated within a community who are least likely to return questionnaires. As local surveys are becoming more common people appear to be more reluctant to give their time to completing them, unless they can be persuaded that it is in their interest. Luckily, there are things you can do to improve the response rate, such as those shown in Figure 7.2.

Be clear about the survey and its aims
- Include a cover letter which clearly explains the reason for the survey
- Provide a date to return the survey
- Stress that the survey is confidential, and that the data will be made anonymous in the reports

Make the questionnaire attractive and easy to complete
- The questionnaire should be short and to the point (taking more than 15 minutes is excessive)
- Offer assistance to complete them

Make it easy for people to return their questionnaires, for example by:
- providing a pre-paid, addressed envelope
- sending people out to collect questionnaires
- offering an incentive for completion and return, such as the chance to be entered in a prize draw

Where a community contains significant numbers of people for whom English is not their first language, translations of the questionnaire into the appropriate language(s) should be made available.

Figure 7.2 Ways of improving survey response rates

Interview surveys

You can undertake interview surveys either face to face with the respondent in the street, door to door or in other public places such as schools, churches or community centres or, alternatively, you can conduct interviews by telephone. With all interview surveys the interviewer talks directly to the respondent using a **structured questionnaire**, which the interviewer works through with the respondent. This personal contact can help to increase a sense of involvement in the project.

Interview surveys are more flexible than self-completion questionnaires; they provide the opportunity to clarify terms that are not clear and probe for more information. Talking to respondents also provides an opportunity to gather supplementary information about them and their community that aids the interpretation of the data. Interview surveys help to ensure a better response rate as you can include those who might have difficulty reading or writing or are not willing to take the time to complete the questionnaire themselves. This method can also help you to target the survey more accurately at specific types of people to ensure that your responses are representative of the entire community.

However, as you will want respondents to be as representative of the general population as possible (as defined by the census and other secondary data), you will almost certainly have to construct quotas (that is, ensure you interview a set proportion of people within certain age bands, ethnicity groups, gender and so on). While it is usually easy for interviewers to select likely looking people with regard to certain characteristics like gender, it is much more difficult to assess someone's age, let alone their employment status, simply by looking at them. To establish that they are speaking to an appropriate person, interviewers may therefore initially have to ask people whether they conform to the quota characteristics they are looking for using a standard screening question before embarking on the interview. This is not always easy as people may be sensitive about being asked such details. Interviewer training for face-to-face interviewing must address these issues.

There are three further issues to consider in relation to interview surveys. First, you will need to ensure that you have sufficient resources available to cover the cost of training interviewers and possibly for travel (for face-to face interviews) or for telephone charges. Second, interviewing respondents can lead to an element of interviewer bias through subtle means such as the tone of the interviewer's voice or body language. And, third, you should consider the length of the questionnaire. People interviewed in the street or on the phone are less likely to be willing to spend more than a few minutes talking to you, although when conducted house-to-house people may spend a little longer. As a result, your questionnaire will have to be quite short and relatively focused.

Face-to-face interviewing

There are some further issues to consider if your survey involves face-to-face interviews. First, it can often be difficult finding respondents at home and so interviewers may have to return to the same house several times at different times of the day and on different days. Methods for this and for logging returned questionnaires are discussed in Appendix 2. Second, due to the lack of anonymity of interview surveys, the respondent may feel threatened, particularly if the subject is a sensitive one. This may be more acute if the interviewer is also from the same community and is known (however indirectly) by the respondent.

Telephone interviewing

Telephone surveys tend to be more like self-completion surveys in terms of the kinds of questions that can be asked. However, they can be a particularly effective way of reaching a lot of people quite quickly and easily. They also usually give relatively high response rates. You can target more accurately who responds to the survey, and the survey work can easily be monitored. However, there are three main disadvantages to using the telephone as a survey method. First, you may initially encounter problems gathering appropriate telephone numbers; many people are now ex-directory or use answerphones to filter out unwanted calls; others use only mobile phones and some have no phone at all. Although a lot of telephone interviewing that targets the general public must be undertaken in the evening, you may still encounter problems finding certain groups of people at home. Call backs are also often necessary, and this can prove expensive. Second, a lack of face-to-face, personal contact means that it is very difficult to build up a rapport and trust between interviewer and interviewee, and respondents tend to be uneasy about discussing things like their financial status or political attitudes over the telephone. You may therefore obtain less information from a telephone interview than from a face-to-face interview and it would be inappropriate, in most cases, to use a telephone survey for in-depth, qualitative interviewing. The third issue relates to persuading people to be interviewed. It is generally much easier for someone to refuse an unseen 'voice' at the end of a phone than a 'real' person on the doorstep. Interviewer training for telephone surveys should look, in particular, at techniques of persuading people not only to participate but not to hang up.

Managing interview surveys

All surveys require someone or a small group to act as survey coordinators. This is especially important with interview surveys, since the coordinator will have responsibility not only for managing a process – ensuring that things get sent to the right people at the right time – but also managing a group of people. Whether they are paid or not, the survey coordinator will have the major responsibility for ensuring that the interviewers carry out the survey to an acceptable standard and in an appropriate manner, that they have the materials that they require, that they are not put at risk and that they receive appropriate support and management.

Observation

Not all the information that you require need be collected by means of a survey. Another useful method of obtaining detailed information about the community is through observation – looking, listening and recording in a systematic manner. Information on the physical aspects of a geographically defined community can be collected through observation. This might include such issues as land use, the condition of housing, road use, and shops and services available within the community. You can also observe the behaviour of people in public places, which can provide insight into how people experience their community and the difficulties they may encounter in day-to-day life. For example, you might want to observe where people cross the road, where children play, the places where young people congregate and so on. You can also use observation to provide insight into the ways in which members of a community interact with each other, for example at community group meetings or places where people come together informally, such as parent and toddler groups or elderly people's lunch clubs. Observing the meetings of community groups and public meetings convened regarding specific topics can provide valuable information about the everyday concerns of members of the community.

Information on the way in which services are delivered to the community can also be gained from observation. How long do people have to wait to be seen in the housing office? How are young people or people with disabilities treated in the local shops? Do the refuse people take away all the rubbish? At what times of the day do people make most use of the local library?

Much of the information that is obtained through this type of observation exercise will not be amenable to statistical analysis. However, it can provide you with useful insights into the life of the community. Observation also allows you to gather information about groups of people who it is difficult to involve in surveys, such as people who are homeless or young people who abuse various substances. Observation might provide answers to questions such as: Where do they go? Why do they do it? How many are involved?

Some situations, by their very nature, can be observed only once because they are unique events, such as a community group meeting. However, it is also possible to observe some events, in the community over time. In the same way that surveys can be repeated to identify any changes that might have occurred, so it is possible to repeat an observation exercise to see whether any changes have resulted following a new policy initiative. For example, how many stray dogs are there in a community spotted before and after a local campaign of canine awareness?

Techniques of observation

There are essentially two approaches to observation – direct observation and participant observation – reflecting the level of involvement one has with the people or groups under observation. Direct observation allows the researcher to examine the community without his or her presence influencing the behaviour of those being observed; in other words, the aim is simply to watch what is going on without taking any part in the activities. However, this can be quite difficult to achieve. The presence of a researcher at a community group meeting may affect the way in which group members interact with each other. Also, an outsider may misinterpret the meaning of people's actions and behaviour. For example, does the presence of large numbers of people at the local church indicate high levels of religious belief or is it simply the best place for people to meet their neighbours?

Participant observation allows you to understand better the meaning of and motives for people's actions and behaviour. Participant observers do not simply watch what is going on but become involved in the group that they are observing. So a researcher undertaking a participant observer study of a community would not just go along to a parent and toddler group and watch what went on there, but would take his or her own toddler and become an active participant. Obviously, this kind of involvement requires a much longer time-scale, as researchers must build up trust with the groups that they wish to observe. There is also the danger that they may become too involved in what it is they are trying to observe. An outsider may be in a better position to see things that those more closely involved take for granted. A participant observer may become so involved that it becomes very difficult to record events and interpersonal interactions objectively.

Another way of thinking about observation is in terms of the level of conspicuousness of the observer. Here the choice is between overt observation and covert observation. In the former the observer will explain his or her presence and the purpose of the research, and in the latter those being observed will be unaware that they are being observed. We have already stated that the conspicuous presence of an observer may alter or influence the behaviour of those being observed. A police officer recording the speeds of vehicles in a side street, for example, may well have the effect of slowing drivers down. Although this may suggest the need for covert observation there are practical difficulties associated with this, such as not being able to take notes at the time. More importantly, there are ethical issues that need to be addressed, such as confidentiality and breaking people's trust in your assumed identity.

Whichever technique of observation you use, it is important to try to retain objectivity and to record faithfully what you observe. We all see and experience our surroundings and each other constantly; however, that does not mean we observe objectively all that happens. We are usually highly selective in assimilating and translating the vast array of information that reaches our brain through our various senses. Observing the community in this unstructured way can give valuable information and impressions that can be built on using other methods. However, it is important to recognize the kinds of subconscious selections you are making and what you may be missing. It may help, therefore, if you observe in a structured way, having decided beforehand what you want to observe, under a series of categories and recording your observations under these headings.

So far we have indicated a number of ways that you might go about observing the community: standing on street corners with a notepad and pen; spending a day or more in the community centre; joining the local social club; or standing in the queue outside the post office on a Thursday morning. Observation can also include the use of measuring instruments and techniques to record objectively the subject you are observing. There are also a number of other techniques that we and others have found useful when undertaking community profiles, which are described in Figure 7.3.

In-depth data collection

Where the aim is to collect in-depth data then there is a range of techniques available that are broadly modelled on normal conversation but which, like other forms of discussion, have their own implicit or explicit interactional rules. Respondents are involved in answering questions or engaging in a discussion around predetermined topics. This discussion may be conducted through individual interviews, **oral testimony** or group discussions.

Individual in-depth interviews

In-depth interviews involve one person, the interviewer, talking to another person, the respondent. The form of the discussion may be more or less structured but in both cases the aim is to provide an opportunity for the respondent to talk in depth about the topic. A structured interview is based on a standard, prepared questionnaire which the interviewer works through with the respondent. The advantage of this method is that it is easy to compare answers from different people because you have asked them all the same questions. The disadvantage is that it may result in a rather stilted conversation and hence produce less useful information than might otherwise be the case.

A semi-structured interview could be based around a checklist of questions or issues that you want to cover in the course of the discussion without the precise wording of those issues being formulated in advance. An advantage of this method is that it generally leads to a more informal dialogue, which should mean that the interviewee is more forthcoming. However, it

Using video
Going out into a community with a video camera can encourage people to express their views and opinions about their community. You can also capture events graphically as they happen. Films of packs of dogs, children playing on unsuitable sites, people crossing busy roads and anti-social behaviour can all give weight and colour to your community profile or be used in discussion in focus groups or workshops. Alternatively you can set up a video diary in a suitable place to help people express and communicate ideas and opinions. With a little knowledge and skill you can edit the tapes to produce a strong graphic record of those views and events on a DVD, although producing a good recording can be very time-consuming.

Using a street map
In the 1970s, a technique was devised by community workers to help them to understand the issues of importance to a community. The researcher would stand in a busy street, looking puzzled or lost, with a map in hand and stop to talk to passers-by. This can lead to many interesting discussions about the area, the environment and its inhabitants, and produce insights that are less easily obtained using more formal methods.

Community walk
The community walk is a useful way of getting to know a community. Those involved in the profile may want to simply walk around an area making notes and discussing what they see. This can bring a number of benefits: a clearer picture of the community may emerge; issues may be seen more clearly and in context; ideas and opportunities for further research may present themselves. It has the added benefit that encounters with local people may provide opportunities to explain what the profiling exercise is for.

Using measuring and recording instruments
There are many devices that can assist in the process of objectively measuring and recording your observations. You may wish to add to the following list.

- Recording: digital camera, video, tape recorder
- Measuring: damp meter, thermometer, noise meter, pedometer, map and ruler, stopwatch, automatic counter, chemical analysis of polluted water, soil, etc.

Figure 7.3   Some observation techniques

is more difficult to analyse the information, as it will not be in a standard format.

Many of the issues we have identified relating to undertaking interview surveys will also apply to conducting in-depth interviews. They are resource-intensive in terms of people and those people undertaking the interviews will require considerable training. In addition, responses from interviews which include a lot of in-depth or qualitative questions may be difficult to code and analyse. There are three further practical issues that are especially relevant to this kind of method and need considering before undertaking in-depth interviews. First, semi-structured interviews can be quite lengthy, so it is important that the interviewee knows this in advance and has the necessary time available. For this reason, it is advisable to contact the interviewees in advance to arrange appropriately timed appointments. Second, semi-structured interviews, because they are much more like a dialogue, entail interviewers being confident and knowledgeable about the issues under discussion so that they are able to ask appropriate supplementary questions. This is especially important when interviewing professional people or service providers. Third, by their nature, semi-structured interviews are not amenable to recording responses through ticking boxes. It may therefore be necessary for interviewers to tape record interviews as well as making some notes during the interview. The interview should then be written up as soon as possible following completion using both notes and tape recording to remind the interviewer of what was said. However, the interviewer must first get the agreement of the interviewees to tape the interview.

Oral testimony

A different type of personal interview is known as oral testimony, or life history. Within all communities there is a considerable wealth of information that is never committed to paper. Families may have lived for several generations in one community and built up significant knowledge and insight about the area in which they live. Oral testimony is a very useful technique for gaining an insight into people's experiences and perceptions within their community; it can uncover aspects of people's lives and the community which otherwise remain hidden. Oral testimony can also help to address politically and socially sensitive topics, which may be difficult to enquire into using other methods, and its findings are often made more powerful when combined with results from other methods. This technique has been used extensively by local historians exploring the changes in family and community life in Britain and abroad. Recording oral testimonies is often the only way of capturing the detail of some aspects of life that would otherwise disappear without trace. It can highlight the experiences of groups of people going back in time to give a historic context to the community and help to fill in the gaps and explain obscure points in the understanding of a community. (See Figure 7.4 for an example.)

All that is needed is a tape recorder and someone with an interesting story to tell. Oral testimonies may be either researcher-led or informant-led. *Researcher-led* oral testimony involves a list of prompting questions to direct respondents towards the issues felt to be most important for the overall project, whereas the *informant-led* approach involves respondents giving their life history or community memories in an open-ended, unstructured way. Although oral testimony can produce rich and interesting data, it can be a very time-consuming method. Several visits are often necessary to collect one

King's Cross Voices Oral History Project
An example of the successful use of oral testimonies is the King's Cross Voices Oral History Project in London. This project is managed through King's Cross Community Development Trust (KCCDT). It works with community members and local partners in seeking to record people's memories and unique life experiences of the King's Cross area. They believe that oral history is a vital tool in building their understanding of their community's recent past and that the technique is ideally suited to uncovering and sharing the hidden background of the diverse nature of the community within King's Cross.

Figure 7.4   Example of oral testimony

Source: www.kingscrossvoices.org.uk/default.asp

person's testimony as people are often much more open in a second or third discussion than in the first. It is also important to determine from the beginning how the testimonies and other sensitive data will be stored. Testimonies may contain very personal and sensitive information so, like all other data, must be stored securely, with only the researchers having access to it.

Group discussions

Community profiles often deal, wholly or partly, with issues which concern not only individuals but also the community as a whole. You may, therefore, want to adopt a more collective approach to gathering information by using group discussions or group interviews. When discussing issues in a group, people may formulate and articulate views that had previously only been vague ideas, their understanding of issues may be clarified by what others are saying, and new ideas and issues may emerge.

Undertaking group discussions entails very different techniques and skills to individual interviewing. First, an appropriate group has to be brought together. You may want to invite community or voluntary groups to send a certain number of representatives or you might want to organize a discussion with a group of people drawn from a particular street or who are involved in the provision of a certain service to the community. In general, the group should consist of no more than seven or eight people with two facilitators to guide and record the discussion.

The group should meet in an informal, comfortable setting and the meeting should be scheduled to last for about one and a half hours. The role of the facilitator is to introduce the themes for discussion, encourage as many people as possible to participate and ensure that no one in the group dominates the discussion or intimidates others. This requires particular skills and it may be a good idea to try to find someone to fulfil this role who has had experience of doing group work. The other facilitator needs to keep a record of the meeting, including: date and venue of meeting; details of who participated; and points raised in discussion. As with semi-structured interviews, a tape recorder can be useful provided the group members agree to its use. Detailed notes of the meeting, including the facilitators' observations, should be written up as soon as possible after the meeting.

The main drawbacks to group discussions are, first, as they are primarily designed to explore issues, perceptions and attitudes in a qualitative way you will not be able to get quantitative data from them. Second, group discussions can generate considerable information but this information can also be difficult to bring together and analyse. Third, as discussion groups are comparatively small they are rarely representative of a community, so it is not possible to make generalizations about the community as a whole from group discussions alone. Finally, to orchestrate an effective group discussion requires considerable facilitation skills.

Combining methods

Chapter 5 suggests that rather than using just one of these methods, you may want to consider using different methods in combination with each other in order to maximize the advantages and minimize the disadvantages. It is worth remembering that any one method will produce only a partial picture. Therefore, if at all possible, it is helpful to employ more than one method, combining them in such a way that they complement each other and produce a more rounded picture of the community. Mixed-method approaches can also help to maximize the numbers of people consulted as some people will prefer to get involved in one way rather than another. For example, some people may respond to a postal survey whereas others will respond only to a phone survey or a web-based survey.

So, for example, you could use a fairly short postal questionnaire to get some basic quantitative data; use individual interviews to target particular groups that you are especially interested in; and then organize a series of group discussions to discuss in greater depth the findings of the earlier stages of the project and start identifying priorities for action. Or, after initial observations and semi-structured interviews with key workers and community activists to help identify a broad range of issues that are of concern to the community, you could undertake a survey of a carefully constructed sample which will throw more light on the extent of feeling about those issues as well as providing essential details about the characteristics of the population. From the survey a number of key issues may emerge that need further elaboration by means, perhaps, of a series of group discussions. Figure 7.5 describes a **case study** as an example of a mixed-method approach.

Methods for collecting primary data can also be combined with those

A case study is an in-depth examination of one example or instance of a wider phenomenon which makes use of a variety of different methods of enquiry. For example, a survey of a community may show that isolation is a particular problem experienced by older people in that community. You could then use a case study approach to highlight that issue. This might entail an in-depth interview with one or more older people, focusing on the issue of social contact and isolation; interviews with a local GP and social worker to discuss the implications of social isolation for health and well-being; and discussions with appropriate groups about how the issue might be tackled.

Case studies allow the researcher to go beyond the initial identification of issues and provide an elaboration of what those issues mean for individuals within the community. Case studies also add colour and life to a community profile.

Figure 7.5   Case studies

for gathering secondary information, as described in the previous chapter. Figure 7.6 gives an example of this approach.

Service user studies are another possible element of a community profile that make use of a variety of different techniques of data collection. For example, if you are looking at the usage of a community centre, you might start by analysing existing information such as committee minutes, newsletters, annual reports and records of bar profits. You could then conduct a survey of users of the community centre and interview staff, committee members and user group leaders. You may also wish to have a group discussion with existing user groups in order to identify problems, potentials and issues. You could also use observation techniques to record what actually happens in the building throughout the course of a typical day, noting, for example, the length of time people spend in certain parts of the building, the facilities they use and people they contact.

Figure 7.6   Service user studies

Summary of key issues

Information is the foundation of a community profile, whether it takes the form of statistics, opinions, beliefs, traditions, pictures or even poetry. The quality of the information, together with the way in which it is presented, will determine in large part whether or not people find the profile interesting, relevant, useful, startling or just informative. Therefore, you need to give considerable thought to what information you need and how it is to be gathered.

Building on Chapters 5 and 6, this chapter has described some techniques for collecting primary information of relevance to community profiles. Furthermore, we suggest that where possible it is a good idea to make use of a range of different methods so that you end up with different kinds of complementary information about the community, its services and resources and its needs. This information can be collected using a variety of different methods, but the principal ones are surveys, observation and in-depth data collection. In deciding which methods to use, it is important that you are clear about what information is required and why, and that you take account of the practical considerations which will affect your choice and are realistic about what you can manage.

8 Analysing the information

Completion of the fieldwork or data collection stage of your project will lead you into the next stage – making sense of the data you have collected, or **data analysis**. Moving from a pile of questionnaires, interview notes and photos to useful information requires a number of different processes. These are, in order, preparing, storing, analysing and presenting the data. These processes are necessary whether you intend to sort, store and analyse your data manually or use a computer, and whether your data is predominantly quantitative or qualitative.

You can start to prepare and analyse your data before you have collected all of it. The results of that analysis may well inform how you go about collecting other information and other questions you may like to ask. Also how you go about analysing your data may influence the methods you choose to use in that data collection. It is therefore important to look at this chapter and think about the process of collating and analysing your material before you start to collect it.

In this chapter, we begin by reviewing the options open to you in relation to data analysis. We then take you through the processes of preparing, storing, analysing and presenting first quantitative data then qualitative data. Finally we discuss the use of computers in handling data. This chapter will provide you with the basic information you need to be able to use the data obtained from a community profiling exercise without providing in-depth knowledge of statistical techniques as such.

Reviewing options for analysing data

Community profiles typically contain a wide range of material drawn from a number of different sources. At the end of the data collection phase you may very well find yourself confronted with a large amount of very different materials including handwritten notes, questionnaires, photographs, minutes of meetings, reports, tape recordings, maps and diagrams. Analysis of this material can be undertaken in a number of different ways although most make use of similar basic processes whereby the material is prepared, then stored in some way before being analysed and then presented in an appropriate format (see Figure 8.1).

Although the next sections of this chapter explore the process of preparation and analysis first of quantitative data and then of qualitative data, the distinction between them is not always clear. Although the use of numbers (quantitative data) may appear to make the data more precise or accurate, words (qualitative data) can give more detail. However, neither on its own gives the whole picture; therefore questionnaires usually ask both closed and **open questions** (the latter needing to be analysed qualitatively), and interviews can be analysed by identifying the number (quantity) of interviewees who think in certain ways or have other common attributes.

Storing and analysing both qualitative and qualitative information can be done either manually or using a computer. In deciding which method to use, you will need to take account of the following considerations: the size of the survey; the type of questions asked and the type of analysis required; the equipment you have available; and the skills that exist within your project group. These issues should have been considered at the beginning of the project and certainly at the time that the questionnaire was designed (see Chapter 6). Failure to make decisions at the planning stage can result in problems later. For example, if you have used a long questionnaire with a very large sample, it will be virtually impossible to analyse the information without a computer. If you did not take account of this before you started, you may well end up with a large pile of questionnaires which you cannot effectively analyse.

Computer analysis requires a computer, appropriate software and people with the skills to use it. Computer packages have become well-established tools in undertaking surveys; they vary in their function, complexity and

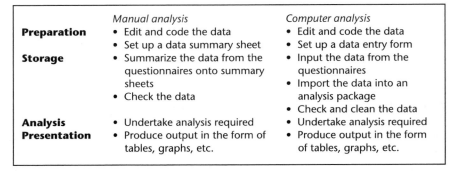

	Manual analysis	Computer analysis
Preparation	• Edit and code the data	• Edit and code the data
	• Set up a data summary sheet	• Set up a data entry form
Storage	• Summarize the data from the questionnaires onto summary sheets	• Input the data from the questionnaires
		• Import the data into an analysis package
	• Check the data	• Check and clean the data
Analysis	• Undertake analysis required	• Undertake analysis required
Presentation	• Produce output in the form of tables, graphs, etc.	• Produce output in the form of tables, graphs, etc.

Figure 8.1   From data to information: processes

sophistication so you will need to look carefully at which one suits your budget and expertise. Later in this chapter we look briefly at some packages you may wish to consider; however, we would recommend that you try at least one computer package with some sample data. Most good books on survey techniques will explain the details of using computers, and packages come with detailed manuals; we therefore give only an overview of the process here.

Manual analysis requires little more than person power, time, pens, paper and a calculator. In general, manual analysis is appropriate only where the survey is quite small and for qualitative data (see later section). However, as many community profiles are small scale, and as it is often very rewarding to work directly with the raw data, we take you through more of the details of the processes involved in the manual analysis of data.

Quantitative data

Preparing the data

Having completed your fieldwork, which might perhaps have involved a residents' survey, and got hold of a range of secondary information of a statistical kind, you need to bring it all together, sort it and produce a list of what you have, what format it is in, where it was collected from, how it was collected and when. Having done this you can then proceed to the next stage: preparing the data for analysis. This is especially relevant to data that has been collected by means of a survey of some kind. Whether you intend to analyse this data manually or by computer, it is necessary first to prepare completed questionnaires. This involves *editing* and *coding* which will not only speed up the process of summarizing the data for manual analysis and entering it into a computer but also reduce the chances of error.

The process of *editing* requires checking through all returned questionnaires to ensure there are no obvious mistakes (for example, as a result of someone having misunderstood a question) and that the appropriate questions have been answered. This is especially important if you used a self-completion questionnaire or where the questionnaire involved a large number of filter questions, both of which increase the chances of questions being missed, misinterpreted or completed incorrectly. Any such questions should be clearly identified so that only relevant information is included.

On completion of the editing process, the response to each question should be clear, a consistent approach to different types of responses should have been agreed upon and there should be no omissions. At this point, coding can begin. It is possible to combine the editing and coding processes. However, this may have the effect of reducing the speed of coding.

Coding refers to the assignment of numerical codes to non-numerical responses (such as open-ended questions) so that statistical analysis can take place. In order to do this, you will require a coding frame, which is essentially a list of the possible responses to each question and the numerical value that corresponds to them. Codes must therefore be mutually exclusive. One way of drawing up a coding frame is to take a 10 per cent sample of returned questionnaires and check the range of responses for each question. These can then be listed or grouped as appropriate and numerical values assigned. Where the survey questionnaire has used a large number of **closed questions**, then this is a simple task as the responses are largely given. However, where an open question is asked, such as 'What additional services or facilities would you like to see provided in your community?', the list of responses must be derived from the sample of completed questionnaires and the appropriate code assigned to it. Codes must be exhaustive so you should include a code for 'other' while trying to minimize the number of responses that are included here. Using the coding frame as a guide, the person coding the questionnaire will then need to go through all questionnaires writing the code number for the response next to it, making sure the application of the coding is consistent throughout.

Storing the data

Once edited and coded, the data set will have to be stored in such a way that it can then be analysed. Again it is possible to do this manually or with a computer. If you are intending to analyse the data manually, you will need to record the responses to all questions in such a way that you can make sense of the data set and get it to answer certain questions. This will involve reading through all the questionnaires and recording all the responses on summary sheets. Where the question is closed it will involve totalling the answers, and where the questions are open it will involve writing down the answers on a summary sheet. Figure 8.2 gives examples of some survey questions with the codes identified. Figure 8.3 shows how this information could be recorded manually using a summary sheet.

In the example summary sheet in Figure 8.3, each respondent has been given a unique number (shown in the first column) which should be written on the questionnaire and can serve two purposes. First, it allows responses to be matched to questionnaires. This may be important if any inconsistencies are discovered in the data. It can also be used for analysis purposes. In the example, we have created a respondent number with three parts: the first is a continuous number to distinguish between respondents; the second records the gender of the respondent; and the third is a code for age. Using the information from the summary sheets, it is a relatively easy task to work out how many men and women, respectively, say they are satisfied with a particular service or whether people in any one age group are more likely than others to express satisfaction or dissatisfaction.

Responses to open questions which cannot be assigned a numerical code

1   Would you like to see more services provided in your area? (CIRCLE ONE)
    Yes   1
    No   2

2   If you have used any of the following services, please say how satisfied you
    are with them? (CIRCLE ONE RESPONSE FOR EACH LINE)

Home care	Very satisfied	Satisfied	Dissatisfied	Very dissatisfied	Don't know
Social worker	Very satisfied	Satisfied	Dissatisfied	Very dissatisfied	Don't know
Day centre	Very satisfied	Satisfied	Dissatisfied	Very dissatisfied	Don't know

3   How many years have you lived at your current address? (CIRCLE ONE)

    0–10   11–20   21–30   31–40   41–50   51–60   61–70   71–80

4   How old were you at your last birthday? (PLEASE WRITE IN)

5   What additional services or facilities would you like to see in your community?
    (PLEASE WRITE IN)

Figure 8.2   Examples of survey questions

Respondent	Question 1 1 2	Question 2 1 2 3 4 5	Question 3 1 2 3 4 5 6 7	
0l/M/3	1	1	1	
02/F/4	1	1	1	

Figure 8.3   Example of manual data summary sheet

may be more difficult to summarize in this way. Where the responses to open
questions are lengthy and quite varied, then the best method is to write the
responses in full on pieces of paper grouped according to characteristics such
as the gender, age and employment status of the respondent.

   If you are intending to use a computer to undertake the analysis, then
you have a number of choices regarding storage of data. You can either use
an integrated package which has its own data entry module or, alternatively,
you can enter the responses into the computer using a data entry package of
which there are a number. These are software packages designed for the input

of numerical data. Another method is to enter the data into a database or spreadsheet package. (See later section on using computers for storing and analysing data, pp. 104–7.)

Once you have entered the data it is a good idea to run a set of **frequencies** to check that it makes sense. If there are any values or variables that should not be there, you will want to check the original questionnaire and then go into the data entry package and amend the data. It is probably a good idea to check a sample of cases against the original questionnaire to ensure they have been input accurately. If the number of responses is not too large, then the sample should be about 10 per cent.

Analysing the data

Once stored in coded format either on a summary sheet or in a computer file, the data can be analysed. Essentially, what is meant by data analysis is getting the data to answer certain questions. Quantitative data enables you to ask questions about things that you feel are most significant; you are usually asking how many, or what proportion. In addition, you can ask questions about the relationships between variables or items of information. In deciding what kinds of analysis you want to do, you will need to consider two main issues: what questions are you trying to answer, and how many variables will you want to look at simultaneously?

In any community profile, there are certain questions which you will almost certainly want to ask of your data. The most basic information is the number and percentage of people who responded in particular ways to each question that was asked in the survey. These are called frequencies (see below). In addition you will almost certainly want to ask questions about the responses of particular groups of people categorized by, for example, age, gender, ethnicity, employment status and so on. Beyond this basic information, you will need to think what other issues you want to address in your analysis. For example, you might want to test a hypothesis about a particular phenomenon, for example is it true that older people are more concerned about crime and personal security than other people? Again your ability to do this is greatly enhanced if you have access to a computer and appropriate software.

One of the main issues you will have to address is how many variables you want to include in your analysis. To count the number of respondents who are male and female and to present that information as a numerical value or as a percentage is termed univariate analysis. However, you may also want to look at the relationship between two variables, for example gender and qualifications. This is called bivariate analysis and would enable you to say, for example, that 33 per cent of women respondents have no formal qualifications. However, you may also want to look at the relationship between more than two variables – that is, multivariate analysis. This would enable you to make statements like: '90 per cent of women with no qualifications have an annual income of less than £5000'. The more variables involved, the more complex the analysis. It is therefore important to decide what level of analysis is appropriate to the aims, objectives and overall purpose of your profile. (Further information about different kinds of analysis can be found in Appendix 2.)

Presenting the data

Statistical data can often be very difficult to interpret, absorb and understand. However, there are a number of different ways in which statistical information can be presented that make data easier to understand. 'The most important rule in communicating quantitative information is to THINK CLEARLY. If you know exactly what your data say you will have little difficulty in communicating the message effectively' (Chapman 1986: 20). In other words, in order to convey statistical information to others, you must understand what it means yourself and also know what is important and what is not. There are three main ways of presenting quantitative information: tables, graphs or charts, and words. Which of these you use will depend on the type of information that you are trying to communicate. Chapman notes that 'tables are best for conveying numerical values, pictures are best for conveying qualitative relationships and words are best for conveying implications for action' (Chapman 1986: 11). A table is essentially a way of summarizing numerical or statistical information. However, some people are put off reading a report if it contains too many tables. Any table that you use should be necessary and clear and should be referred to in the text. Figure 8.4 (overleaf) makes some general points about tables.

Charts are graphical ways of demonstrating the relationship between variables. The three types of chart that you are most likely to find useful are pie charts, line graphs and bar charts. Figure 8.5 (overleaf) makes some general points of relevance to all three kinds of charts.

Pie charts are particularly useful in demonstrating the relative proportions of sub-groups making up a whole. For example, Figure 8.6 (p. 101) is a pie chart which shows the proportions of a survey response sample who have been resident at their current address for different lengths of time. Line graphs are useful for highlighting changes over time. For example, Figure 8.7 (p. 101) shows the monthly figures for reported crimes over a year. From this graph, it is very easy to see that the crime figures dipped sharply in July and August to rise again in September. Bar charts can be used to show the relative size of groups and changes over time and, in addition, can be used to illustrate the relationship between two or more variables. For example, Figure 8.8 (p. 102) is a bar chart showing the number of respondents expressing satisfaction with a number of different services. From this chart, it is easy to see that the housing office attracted more dissatisfied responses than did social workers or GPs.

Every table should:
- contain enough information so that it can be read on its own
- have a consecutive number and an appropriate title
- use a standard format
- be discussed in the text to reinforce the message
- be carefully selected (is it really necessary?)
- have rounded figures to demonstrate a point
- have figures in columns to aid comprehension and mental arithmetic
- order categories by size so that the largest or most significant is first
- use footnotes to explain or qualify any figures or sections
- provide a reference to its source if it is not primary data
- have figures being compared in columns
- break up long columns – groups of five are suggested

Figure 8.4 General points about tables

Charts should:
- be numbered and have an appropriate title
- be discussed in the text
- show units and scales of measurement
- not include too much information
- have 'graphical integrity', i.e. represent what they are supposed to represent
- be easy to read and interpret

Figure 8.5 General points about charts

A community profile can be considerably enhanced by appropriate use of tables, graphs and charts. However, they will still require comment in the written part of the report. You will need to refer to them and draw the reader's attention to the key point that they are being used to demonstrate and also draw out the implications from them.

Qualitative information

If your primary research involves in-depth interviews, focus groups or public meetings, then the type of analysis required will be different to that for a self-completion questionnaire or a structured interview. As with quantitative analysis, one can analyse qualitative data either manually or using a computer

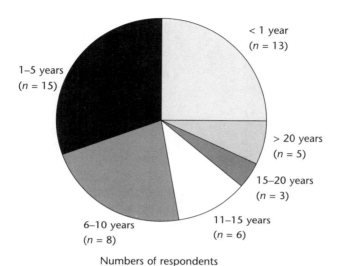

Figure 8.6   Example of a pie chart

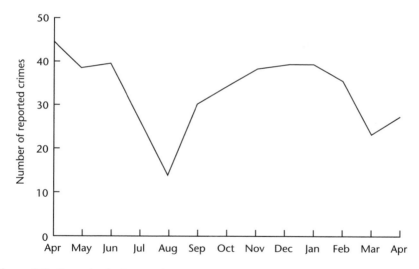

Figure 8.7   Example of a line graph

package. Computer packages for analysing qualitative information are less common than those for use in analysing quantitative data, but the selection is growing. As a general rule, if the survey involves long, semi-structured interviews with a large sample, then using a computer package will aid the analysis and make it more efficient. We describe the use of computers in the analysis of

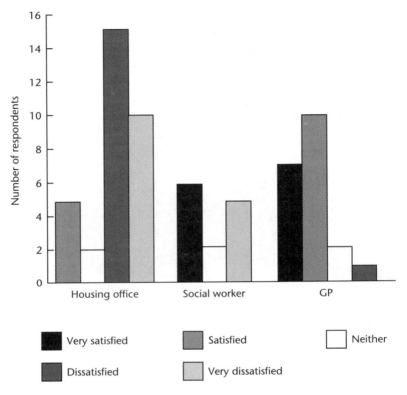

Figure 8.8 Example of a bar chart

qualitative data in the next section; here we describe the process of manual analysis of qualitative data. As with quantitative data analysis it is necessary to go through similar stages in the process.

Preparing and storing the data

How should one begin to analyse a range of qualitative material without using a computer? There are two initial tasks: first, the material may be in the form of handwritten notes or on tape. It is possible to analyse directly from these formats; however, it is generally much easier if notes are typed up using a word-processing package. And, second, each interview or group discussion transcript must be assigned a unique number.

The material is then annotated. This can be done by writing in the margins of reports, underlining or highlighting on hard copies key phrases in interview transcripts, or highlighting sections of a document in a word processor. The annotations are intended to highlight those points that you consider are the most important, key themes or perhaps possible quotes you can use in a final report.

In another copy of the document, or using another colour on the same copy, you can then code certain key passages in a similar way to the coding process described in the section on quantitative data. A number of different coloured highlighting pens are useful for marking passages. You may already have key themes in mind and have worked out a coding frame that you will apply to the texts or you may want to develop the coding frame on the basis of an initial review of the material itself.

Analysing the data

Having read through the qualitative data, annotated and coded it, it then needs to be 'deconstructed'. There are a number of ways in which this can be carried out; you could take each question separately or take groups of questions within one theme altogether. A simple way of doing this involves the careful use of a pair of scissors to cut up the written information according to questions, main themes or issues. Make sure you use photocopied documents if they have not been transcribed on a word processor. Each piece of paper should have the respondent's unique identification number written on it so that the source of the information can be traced back to the original. It is also useful to make a note of the respondent's characteristics (age, gender, ethnicity, etc.) if these are not already part of the identification number.

Once the data has been sorted in this way, you should be able to read through all the material noting the key and related issues and bearing in mind the context in which particular comments have been made. Analysis can then proceed by means of grouping similar issues or themes together and then, if necessary, further dividing and subdividing these categories. Some of these emerging concepts can then be further tested with other individual or group interviews. Overall the purpose of the exercise is to explore the data in such a way that you can identify patterns of responses.

Presenting the data

Once you have identified the main themes and hierarchies of themes, and explored possible explanations for patterns of responses, you need to find clear ways of presenting your findings. One way qualitative data can be presented is through summarizing what has been said in relation to particular themes or issues and indicating what is the majority view and outlining other, alternative views.

Alternatively, or in addition, in presenting the findings from this analysis you could use particularly significant examples of individuals or groups that illustrate interesting, atypical or representative issues or themes that you have identified. You may for example want to highlight the actions of a particular agency that you are arguing is characteristic of other agencies or use a quote to illustrate a minority perspective. Again it is important not to take such cases out of context.

Equally important might be the judicious use of photographs and other illustrations. The adage 'every picture tells a story' means that one photograph can reinforce your message if not make it for you, whilst another could undermine it. Pictures therefore not only add interest to pages of script (especially if they depict people) but can also be used to illustrate points in ways that words and statistics are unable to do.

Using computers to analyse data

The use of computers in survey research and statistical analysis is now commonplace and, indeed, many books on survey research do not even consider manual analysis of data. In considering survey software you have essentially two choices. You can either buy the software and do the work yourself, or you can use one of the online software hosting sites; these let someone else take care of most of the details for you. An internet search will reveal a range of current sites that offer this service for a range of prices.

If you buy and install your software on your own computer you will need to know how to use the software package and have the time to input the findings and analyse the results. There are many packages on the market which can be used in survey research and which vary in price and sophistication. Whichever software package is used, the procedures for storing and analysing the data will be similar.

There are software packages for inputting data, analysing data and producing graphical output, and some integrated packages that perform all the functions required for survey analysis. Before choosing a package, you will need to consider the issues indicated in Figure 8.9. If you have little or no knowledge of computer packages, then ease of use, a telephone helpline, menu system and good documentation will be especially important in selecting the appropriate software package.

Dedicated profiling programs

There are two main packages that have been designed specifically for undertaking community profiles. These are both packages that provide the software to take you through the data collection, entry and analysis stages. If your study is being undertaken in a rural area, you could make use of an integrated package called Village Appraisal. This software package is designed specifically for profiles of small villages or rural areas (see Figure 8.10). The

- Will the software run on your computer?
- Will the software perform all the tasks that you require, e.g. data entry, analysis?
- Will you need optional plug-ins with more features to use?
- Are you able to adjust the settings to your own personal preferences?
- Will it produce the kinds of statistics that you require?
- Can the software package cope with the size of your data set?
- How much can you afford to spend?
- Is there telephone and/or online support?
- Is the software user-friendly?
- Does the package include training?
- Are the manuals easy to use?

Figure 8.9   Issues to consider when selecting a software package

Village Appraisal is an integrated software package which contains three 'units'.

1 CREATE creates a questionnaire from a database of 400 questions from which the user can select up to 80 questions; in addition, a limited number of questions specific to the community under study can be included; the questionnaire is then printed out

2 DATAIN allows the user to enter the responses to the questions

3 ANALYSE undertakes the analysis and prints the results in either graphical or tabular form; the analysis consists of frequencies for each question and some multivariate analysis is also possible; a basic report is produced which can be imported into a word-processing package

This package has the advantage of being relatively cheap and it can save a great deal of time as it is integrated and easy to use. The main drawback is that it is limited in terms of the analysis that can be performed. However, in most cases, it will probably be sufficient.

For further information: www.glos.ac.uk/faculties/ccru/village-appraisal/index.cfm

Figure 8.10   Village Appraisal integrated software package

other package, which is designed for urban and other areas, is Compass (see Figure 8.11, overleaf).

Statistical analysis software packages

It is possible to use database or spreadsheet packages (such as Access or Excel) for certain stages of the research process. They tend to be limited in terms of data analysis but can be useful for data entry. Once the data set has been

Compass for Windows is a software package designed to assist those who wish to carry out research but who may not have all of the specialist skills required. Developed from the original 1996 version, Compass for Windows brings together the main elements of primary research to form an integrated, user-friendly software package enabling agencies and individuals to conduct social audits or community profiles in their local areas. The package is extremely flexible and has been designed to be easy to understand and use. It is designed to assist in three elements of the research process.

1 Questionnaire design: design your questionnaire from over 400 fully editable questions organized into several categories. Add an unlimited number of your own questions and interviewer instructions as required. Print your questionnaire in A4 or booklet format.
2 Data processing: no need to design a separate data entry form. Compass for Windows automatically sets out the screen for the user to input direct from completed questionnaires.
3 Data analysis: produce frequency counts, cross-tabulations and text analysis at the touch of a button. Results of analysis can be presented in numeric or graphical form (pie charts or bar graphs) and can be copied straight into your other Windows-based software.

For further information contact: pri@leedsmet.ac.uk

Figure 8.11   Compass community profiling software

entered, it can then be imported into another package for statistical analysis such as SPSS, Statgraphics or Minitab. In addition there are several integrated packages that you might want to consider; these vary in price and sophistication. Possibly the most commonly used software package for survey research is Statistical Package for the Social Sciences (SPSS). SNAP is another integrated package designed for survey analysis. Like the dedicated packages described earlier, it employs a menu system and is easy to use for the simple analysis of survey data. (For further information see the resources listed in Appendix 3.)

There is also an increasing range of software packages available that are designed to assist with qualitative data analysis. Computer Assisted Qualitative Data Analysis Software (**CAQDAS**), as these packages are sometimes called, vary in function although they work in essentially the same way as we have described manual analysis. The first task is to type all the text into a word-processing program. Once the text has been checked, it is saved in a format ready for import into a package. At this stage you will need to print it out and decide which sections are important. These sections then have to be coded as described earlier. Codes can be stored and manipulated in the program (adding, deleting, merging, ordering and even weighting them). Once this process is complete, the data can be analysed.

If you intend to use a qualitative analysis package, you should be prepared to invest considerable resources in terms of both time and money. Because the process is resource-intensive it is probably not worth making the investment for relatively small numbers of interviews. However, a project that contained a large qualitative element would be difficult to undertake using manual methods of analysis.

Summary of key issues

Analysing data is generally easier to do than read about. Most community profiles can be produced using only frequencies and some **cross-tabulations**, with perhaps some verbatim comments drawn from interviews or group discussions and some well-chosen photographs. Analysing data manually need not be too daunting and can prove interesting and enlightening, and, if done collectively, can be enjoyable. If an integrated package such as Compass for Windows or Village Appraisal is used, then this process can be quite straightforward. In deciding whether to analyse data manually or using a computer, and in considering which software package to use, you will need to consider how large your survey is, what analysis is required, what expertise you have and what resources are available.

Reference

Chapman, M. (1986) *Plain Figures*. London: HMSO.

9 Maximizing impact

The most thoughtfully planned, systematically executed and carefully analysed community profile will have little or no impact unless it is also effectively communicated. Communication involves more than one person giving another person information. It involves, at least, one person conveying a message and another receiving and understanding that message. Fulfilling that objective is likely to require more than simply writing and disseminating a report.

Communication, as with all other elements of the profiling process, needs to be planned in advance. Consideration will need to be given to what you are trying to achieve through your community profile; who are the different audiences for it; and what might be the best way of communicating with them. In practice the most effective communication or engagement strategies start right at the beginning of the profiling process, for example by involving key stakeholders in the steering group and in the design of the profile and by keeping them informed during the process through interim reports or briefings. If you adopt this approach then your audience is already prepared to receive the findings once they are available and may feel some ownership of them.

This chapter starts by looking at the types of impact that might be achieved through a community profile. It then takes you through the process of deciding what kind of impact you are trying to achieve and the audiences that you are trying to reach. Finally we look at some different ways in which you might engage with these different audiences in order to achieve your desired impact. You may want to use the template in Figure 9.1 as a way of organizing your ideas about communication and dissemination activities.

Types of impact

A community profile, as with other kinds of research, can have a range of different types of impact. First, it might have an impact on people's *understanding*.

What kinds of impacts do you want your profile to have?	Who are the possible users of or audiences for the profile?	Contextual issues that need to be taken into account	What are the best ways of engaging with these audiences?	Actions

Figure 9.1   Template for planning engagement activities

For example, as a result of carrying out the community profile local people might have a better understanding of the composition of the local population or the white population might have a better understanding of the issues faced by minority ethnic groups. Or ward councillors and council officers might have a better understanding of residents' attitudes towards local services.

Second, your community profile could have an impact on people's *attitudes*. For example, a better understanding of the needs and aspirations of young people in a locality might result in a change of attitude towards them on the part of older local residents. Or by highlighting the positive aspects of a community and its residents your profile might have the effect of changing other people's perceptions of a local area that has had a poor image and reputation in the past.

More tangibly, a community profile that highlights particular local needs or gaps in services might have an impact on local *policy* by changing the pattern of resource or service allocation. In other words, the council might take the decision to provide more or better services or services that better meet the needs of local people. Similarly, a community profile which demonstrates dissatisfaction with the way in which local services are delivered might encourage local agencies or individuals with a responsibility for providing local services to change the way in which they do things so that services are delivered more effectively.

In some cases the aim of the community profile is to *persuade*. This is especially relevant to organizations that undertake profiling exercises in order to support a bid for funding. In this case the community profile is used to demonstrate the nature and extent of local needs or to demonstrate that a new service or facility would be used by local people.

It is often true that community profiles are undertaken as part of a wider process of *community development*. In such cases the process of doing the community profile will have been used as a means of developing a greater understanding of the strengths and difficulties within the community, bringing the community together, developing skills and building capacity or celebrating the history and diversity of a local area. In such cases the findings from the community profile are likely to be used as the basis for developing community action that takes forward the community development process.

What kind of impact are you trying to achieve?

In planning a strategy for maximizing the impact of your community profile you will need to refer back to your original purpose and aims and objectives in order to determine which of these kinds of impact you are trying to achieve. Of course, it is quite likely that you will want to effect a number of different kinds of changes and it is worth trying to disentangle exactly what these are. One way of doing this is to think about the possible audiences for the community profile and what kind of an impact you would like to achieve with each of them. The audiences that you will want to reach are likely to be the same stakeholders that you identified early on in the profiling process (see Chapter 4), including:

- local residents – you may need to think about different groups within the local community that are especially relevant;
- community organizations;
- agencies delivering local services, e.g. GP, schools, local shops, housing associations, voluntary organizations;
- elected representatives – ward councillors, MP;
- local council or particular departments within the council;
- other organizations with oversight for local services, e.g. PCT, Local Education Authority.

Figure 9.2 lists some questions that you might want to consider in determining the possible audiences for your profile.

In thinking about these potential audiences it is also worth considering the contexts in which they are operating that might have implications for how and when you engage with them about your community profile. For example, around local election time you may want to talk to candidates about their response to the issues raised by your community profile in the hope that one

Issues to consider

- Who/what are the individuals or agencies that you are trying to influence?
- What kinds of relationships do you already have with these individuals/groups? Can you build on these?
- What are the relationships between these groups? Do they have common or overlapping interests?
- Are any of these groups particularly important in relation to leverage or influence?
- Are there 'intermediary' or 'gatekeeping' individuals or organizations that might be helpful to you?

Figure 9.2   Who are the likely audiences for your profile?

or more of them will take them up as part of their campaign. Conversely, election time is a bad time to try to engage with council officers as they will not make any major decisions, especially those requiring changes in patterns of resource allocation or service delivery, in advance of an election. Take advantage, if you can, of other issues that are currently on the agenda locally and try to relate the findings of your community profile to those issues. For example, if the local crime rate has been a matter for local debate or has featured in the local press then you might be able to use this as a 'hook' on which to hang some of your findings and to seek publicity for them. All local authority areas have to produce a Community Strategy that sets out priorities for the area covered (city, district, county). You might be able to link the issues facing your community with these wider, local priorities and gain some leverage that way.

What kinds of output are likely to have the most impact?

When considering what kinds of methods to use to engage with your audiences it is important to remember that, while you may feel that the findings from your profile are interesting, informative, convincing and useful, others may need to be persuaded that this is the case. Different audiences will respond in different ways to different forms of communication and so you will need to tailor the outputs from your profile to those specific audiences. This will almost inevitably mean that you will have to produce more than one output and also think about engaging with the same audience in a number of different ways in order to make sure that they get your message. Studies of what works in relation to research impact have shown that adopting a 'multi-method' approach to communicating findings is often more effective than using a single method. Similarly, effective communication is generally active and two-way. In other words, simply sending someone a report that they are then required to read is a passive, one-way form of communication, whereas inviting someone to a workshop where they have the opportunity to discuss the findings and think through the implications is more active and two-way, and likely to be more effective. The issues that you need to consider are summarized in Figure 9.3 and a list of possible ways of engaging can be found in Figure 9.4. It is important to remember that there is no right or wrong way of communicating; rather you need to match the kind of influence that you are trying to have on a certain audience with the form of engagement that is best suited to that objective.

- Are you more likely to have an impact through *direct* or *indirect* forms of engagement?
- Is your preferred form of engagement *active, passive* or *interactive*?
- Should you *target* your output to a small number of carefully selected individuals or would it be better to disseminate more widely?
- Will your target audiences respond better to *written, verbal, electronic* or some other form of communication?
- Do you want the output from your community profile to be a *permanent* record or will something with a shorter shelf-life suffice?
- What *budget* do you have available for this phase of the work?
- Are you aiming for something with *high initial impact* or something that *invites longer-term consideration*?

Figure 9.3 Issues to consider when deciding on forms of engagement

So, in relation to specific audiences you may want to consider a phased programme of engagement using a number of different methods (see Figure 9.5 for an example). In setting your aims and objectives you will, at the beginning of the profiling process, have considered audiences and possible impacts. At this stage it is a good idea to get key people involved, for example in a steering group, so that they feel some ownership of the profile and have had some input into the process. If this has happened then it is more likely that the person concerned will take note of the findings when they receive them.

Written reports

It is generally a good idea to produce a single, comprehensive document that details all your findings and the methods that you used; this will be your core document that other outputs will draw on. Even if you decide that this report is not going to be widely circulated it is still worth thinking about how best to present the information that it will contain. Whoever the audience is there are

Events
- (Spoken) presentation at someone else's event
- (Spoken) presentation at your own event
- Seminar
- Workshop
- Training

Written outputs
- Press report
- Written report
- Summary
- Leaflet
- Newsletter
- Toolkit
- Letters/emails

Other media
- Video/DVD
- CD
- Display/exhibition
- Formal/informal conversations
- Website

Figure 9.4   Possible ways of engaging

Target audience: ward councillors
Impact that you want to achieve: increase their awareness of the needs of young people in your local community and lobby for better youth service provision
Methods
- Enlist them in the steering group for the community profile
- Keep them informed of progress while the work is going on, through short briefings
- When the profile is completed, send them a copy of the summary report together with a personalized letter highlighting the key issues
- Follow this up with an invitation to a workshop to discuss the implications of the report
- After the workshop write to thank them for attending and summarize the actions that you would like them to take on your behalf

Figure 9.5   Example of engagement strategy

a number of good practice principles that you should think about. These are as discussed below.

Accessibility

Make sure that you write using simple, clear, appropriate language avoiding slang, jargon and clichés, and spelling out abbreviations. If you find that you are using a lot of words or acronyms that are quite technical you may want to consider including a short glossary. Be precise, avoiding vague or ambiguous words and expressions. The need for clarity in writing style is well expressed by Kane (1985: 176):

> If your audience is your local residents' association, parents' group or club, you probably know their 'language' as well as anyone. Most people today are too busy to waste time wading through jargon. On the other hand, forced informality or heavy-handed chattiness can be equally annoying. Do not write 'down' and do not try to get the approval of your audience by using their in-group dialect or slang if you are not a member of the group. Older people who try to use teenagers' 'in-words', for example, can look foolish and alienate their audience. Clear, concise, understandable writing should be your aim.

Finding relevant information

Not everyone will read the report from beginning to end; most people will want to focus on the sections in which they are most interested. Think about a logical structure for the report and help readers find their way through it by using clear section headings that inform them what each section is about. Include a detailed contents page. (See Figure 9.6 for an example of a standard report structure.)

Making it easy to read

Think about the layout of your report. Select a clear font in a point size that is easy to read and make sure you don't overcrowd the page; include wide margins to create a 'clean' look. If you have access to a colour printer and/or photocopier think about how you can use colour to improve the appearance of the report, for example by having different-coloured headings or using colour in graphs, tables and illustrations. If you do not have access to colour printing and copying, change the appearance of the font to break up the text on the page, for example by using bold or italics or a different-sized font for headings.

- *Title page* – Name of the report. You might want to use a title that captures the imagination, for example a telling phrase from your interviews or questionnaires, or it might be a more straightforward description of what the report is about. If you go for the former then add a more descriptive 'strapline' as well, e.g. 'Anytown: a community profile'. The title page should also include the names of the authors and/or the group that has produced the report, who published it and the date.

- *Summary* – This is aimed at those people who do not have the time or interest to read the whole document. The summary should consist of the key findings together with enough background information for the reader to make sense of the findings.

- *Acknowledgements* – An opportunity to thank those who have contributed in some way to the production of the community profile. This might include council officials who provided secondary data, those who participated in community discussions, people who responded to a survey and anyone who gave advice or assistance with the process. It is vital that you don't leave anyone out and that names are spelt correctly.

- *Contents page* – This is vital to help people navigate their way around the report so include headings, sub-headings and page numbers. You may also want to include a separate list of tables and charts.

- *Introduction* – This should include the background to the project (how it came about), the context, terms of reference and aims and objectives and some details about methodology (how you went about undertaking the profile) and sources of information. If you have undertaken a survey you should give details about your sample – how it was derived, how it compares with the population as a whole – and the response rate. If you have undertaken group discussions or meetings, you should describe how these were organized and structured.

- *Body of report divided into appropriate sections* – Your findings will comprise the main part of the report organized by theme or topic. You may find it helpful to go back to your original aims and objectives in order to identify the key questions that you were seeking to answer and use this as a framework for organizing your material. It is good practice for each section to begin with an introductory paragraph outlining the scope and content of the section and to finish with a brief summary of key points.

- *Conclusions and recommendations* – These should follow logically from the findings in the body of the report. You may want to summarize the key issues and identify the priority issues. Where appropriate this can then lead on to recommendations or action points.

- *References* – Cluttering the text with detailed references to the sources you have used can make the report difficult to read. However, it is good practice to note the sources used. An annotated bibliography or 'Notes on sources' may be more useful than a simple listing of references.

- *Appendices* – Appendices are generally used for technical information or copies of documents that it would be inappropriate to include in the main part of the report. For example, you may want to put detailed data tables into an appendix together with copies of questionnaires or interview schedules used.

Figure 9.6 Standard report structure

Highlighting key messages

Make sure that the reader's eye is drawn to the key messages that you want to communicate. You can do this through the use of checklists, boxed inserts, headings and sub-headings, and the use of different fonts including bold and italics.

Using evidence to support your statements

Ensure that any statements you make are supported by the findings from your profile. You will damage your credibility if you make generalizations or sweeping statements that are not supported by evidence. Findings can be reinforced by suitable illustrations and examples including case histories, quotations and photographs. (See also Chapter 8.)

Written summaries

It is likely that very few people will read your report from cover to cover. So, in addition to the full report you will need to produce a summary that conveys the main points. The summary is often included as a preface to the main report as well as being produced as a 'stand-alone' document. You need to think carefully about who the main audiences for this will be and try to produce it in such a way that it will fulfil a number of different functions. For example, you may want to distribute it to local residents as a means of feeding back findings from the profile. You may also want to use it to draw people in to follow-up work such as action planning or discussion groups. In addition you may want to send it to local service providers, council officers and elected representatives.

A summary leaflet should be short and attractively produced and succinctly convey the key messages. It should also give contact details so that those who are interested can seek out further information. The Joseph Rowntree Foundation's *Findings* series is a good model to emulate (Joseph Rowntree Foundation 2006). These follow the same basic structure, covering no more than four sides of A4. On the first page you will find a short introductory paragraph followed by a bulleted list of key findings, usually no more than ten. On the inside two pages the background to the research is briefly outlined followed by a more detailed exposition of the findings and a concluding paragraph. On the final, back page there is a short paragraph entitled 'About the project' that briefly describes the methods used, followed by a section that gives bibliographic details for the report, including where it can be obtained.

If the primary audience for your summary is the local community then you might feel that something even shorter is more appropriate, perhaps produced as a leaflet or a newsletter that includes photographs or pictures.

The process of report writing

Producing a report involves bringing together material from a wide range of different sources. This might include official publications, census data, other official statistics, survey findings and also material obtained from interviews with members of the community, service providers, policy makers and community representatives and notes from group discussions or public meetings. You may also have maps, photographs, graphs, charts and tables. Your task in writing the report is to bring together this diverse material in such a way that it is easy to read and conveys certain key messages while remaining faithful to the sources of evidence that you are using. This is not an easy process. The following principles may help:

- *Refer back to the research questions* and use these to generate themes around which to structure your material (see Chapter 5).
- *Be selective* in your use of material; you do not have to include all the data that you have collected but make sure that you don't exclude anything that is of interest, or reflects an important viewpoint, or provides conclusive evidence.
- *Combine quantitative and qualitative data:* for example, you may want to provide the statistical data in relation to a particular issue and then illustrate what this means for the community by including a quotation from an interview with a local resident (see Chapters 6 and 8).
- *Present statistical data in accessible ways:* statistical data can be difficult to understand and absorb; think about using graphs or charts as an alternative to tables (see Chapter 8).
- *Be faithful to your sources:* make sure that you don't unintentionally (or intentionally) introduce a bias into your report by giving certain viewpoints more attention than others or by omitting certain bits of information. A key test is to ask yourself the following questions. What is the evidence in support of this statement? Is there any conflicting evidence to which I should draw attention?
- *Try to use the 'PEE' structure:* this refers to making your Point, citing the Evidence in support of it and then providing some Explanation of what it means.

Electronic publication

Increasingly people expect to be able to access information using electronic means. If you have a website for your organization then this might involve providing a link from the website to your report or summary that allows people to download and print them. This, of course, has the added advantage of reducing the use of paper and reducing costs. In addition, email can be a very effective means of rapidly and cheaply either alerting key people to the existence of the report and/or sending it to them as an attachment.

Alternative ways of presenting information

You may feel that presenting your findings in written format cannot adequately convey what you are trying to say. Increasingly people are turning to alternative media to present information. This might be a CD or DVD which facilitates the inclusion of photographic material and interviews. A display or exhibition might also be another way of getting your message across (see Figure 9.7 for some ideas of where to place a display or exhibition). These kinds of methods can, however, be relatively expensive to produce well and will probably require at least some professional input. You should also remember that, as suggested above, if at least part of your purpose is to present information about your community then whatever method you use to convey that information there does need to be somewhere a detailed record of the findings that underpin the presentation.

- Town hall or other civic buildings
- Library
- School entrance or corridor
- Supermarket
- Launderette
- Youth and community centres
- Art gallery or museum

- JobCentre
- Schools
- Nursery
- Church/faith centres
- Local shops
- Takeaways

Figure 9.7   Possible sites for a display or exhibition

Using the local media

Local newspapers and local radio and television are often very keen to hear about local activities and events. Think about writing a press release that draws attention to your findings and any activities that you are organizing around the profile such as seminars, workshops and **action planning**. However, if you send out a press release you must also be prepared to be interviewed by a local journalist. And, remember, focus on a few key messages that can be clearly and succinctly expressed.

Other kinds of engagement

So far we have talked essentially about one-way communication; you are presenting information to a reader (or, in the case of a CD/DVD, a viewer). However, there is increasing evidence to show that research findings are more likely to have an impact if the recipient becomes an active participant in the process of communication and has an opportunity to engage with the findings that s/he is receiving. Again we need to think about this in terms of the different audiences for the community profile.

Members of the local community might welcome an opportunity to attend a workshop that allows them to hear about the findings from the profile, ask questions and then to engage in some kind of activity that seeks to address the issues raised by the profile. This has the benefit not only of communicating the findings but also moving the process along in terms of action. There are a number of different models that can be used for this kind of event, including action planning (see Figure 9.8). However, there are many different options for community events and activities. The two publications by Wates (1996, 2000) give useful information on these kinds of community-based events and activities.

If your main audience is policy or decision makers in the council or other organizations, then a more formal seminar – for example, a presentation followed by questions and discussion – might be more appropriate. However, you will need to think carefully about who you want to attend this event, and take

---

- It can promote increased participation, both by encouraging activists and leaders, and by involving participants in [activities], such as Planning for Real exercises
- It can involve more local citizens in identifying and prioritizing local needs and engage them in the designing and shaping of individual local public services
- It can stimulate local involvement in the development and ownership of local projects to meet needs and provide a case to support fundraising
- It can influence wider priorities in service delivery and the allocation of resources, including the provision of private-sector services, such as the siting of a supermarket
- It can provide a process for making a lasting difference to the area's social, economic and environmental well-being and for local action to help achieve sustainable development in the wider world
- It can contribute to the growth of neighbourhood governance by generating better local intelligence, and by helping to create community-owned forums through which local people can express their views

---

Figure 9.8 Benefits of local action planning

Source: Home Office (2004) *Firm Foundations. The Government's Framework for Community Capacity Building.* London: Home Office, p. 23

steps to secure their commitment. You may need to enlist the help of your ward councillors in this process. Think carefully too about the best time of day for such a seminar and the location. Remember that while the community profile is very important to you, it may not be very high up the agenda of managers in organizations and agencies.

Another important audience that you might want to engage is local service providers – the people who deliver services at the frontline in your local area. This might include: GPs, health visitors, headteachers, housing managers, youth workers, college principals and so on. Think about the key messages from your profile that would be useful to these people and focus on those. You may want to think about a lunchtime event for this group where you provide refreshments; people can listen to what you have to say and then have the opportunity to discuss the findings and the implications for their service. Again try to present the event as something that will be helpful to them in their work.

You may feel that a less formal opportunity for people to find out about the profile and to ask questions and discuss the findings is more appropriate. You might consider holding an open day at a local community centre or a series of drop-in sessions at, for example, the local library. An important aspect of this kind of approach is for there to be plenty of things for people to look at, for example display boards that present key information, summary leaflets and so on, and also for people to be asked to engage in some kind of activity. This might be a rolling exercise asking people to rate the importance to them of certain issues, or to propose actions to address specific problems or issues, or a set of statements to which they are asked to respond. At the very least you will need a signing-in sheet so that you have some record of how many people have attended.

In planning events of this kind, some general points are relevant, relating to selection of venues, timing of meetings, accessibility and so on. These have already been discussed in Chapter 4.

Keeping the profile up to date

Producing the community profile, undertaking dissemination and follow-up action-planning activities might be the end point for the community profiling group. The group may disband or may become involved in progressing the actions implied by the profile. Nevertheless, you may want to consider coming together again at some point in the future in order to review the progress that has been made and the changes that have come about as a result of the profiling exercise. It can be very encouraging and rewarding to record improvements made as a result of your efforts. However, change can take a long time to come about. You may also want to review why things are *not* happening as quickly as you had hoped and whether there are any outstanding issues that require further action. You may also want to consider whether further profiling work should be undertaken in the future. After all, any community profile only represents a single snapshot at a particular point in time and will quickly become out of date.

Summary of key issues

While the process of undertaking the community profile is very important, in most cases you will want to produce some kind of output as a record of what you have found out through the profiling process. Furthermore, you will probably want this output to have an impact in terms of changing people's understanding or attitudes and/or policies and practice that affect the locality. Ensuring that your profile has maximum impact will involve careful planning of how you record the information from your profile and what you will do with that record once it has been produced. This in turn entails thinking about the kind of impact you would like to have, who the audiences are for your profile and what might be the best ways of reaching them.

Because audiences are different you will probably have to produce more than one output in order to meet their needs and also to engage with the same audience in different ways at different times in order to reinforce your message. Most community profiles result in some kind of documentary record of the findings. This is typically a written report. It is generally a good idea to produce a written report even if you do not intend to circulate it very widely; it will become the source document that provides the basis from which other, more user-friendly outputs can be developed.

Producing outputs or artefacts from the community profile is only the first step in ensuring that your profile has an impact on your intended audiences. As important or more important are how you distribute these outputs and what else you do to gain people's attention. Face-to-face opportunities for people to discuss the findings from, and implications of, the profile and to participate in action planning are generally more effective in ensuring that your profile has an impact.

References

Joseph Rowntree Foundation (2006) www.jrf.org.uk/knowledge/findings/, accessed 7 November 2006.
Kane, E. (1985) *Doing Your Own Research*. London: Marion Boyars.

Wates, N. (1996) *Action Planning. How to Use Planning Weekends and Urban Design Action Teams to Improve Your Environment*. London: Prince of Wales's Institute of Architecture.

Wates, N. (2000) *The Community Planning Handbook*. London: Earthscan.

10 Conclusions

Over the last decade, since the publication of the first edition of this book, community profiling has, arguably, moved from being a somewhat marginal activity into the mainstream of policy and practice. This has come about because of a number of mutually reinforcing drivers. Central government – first the Thatcher governments and then New Labour – has been preoccupied with how to modernize public services and, in particular, make them more responsive and accountable to those who use them and pay for them. This has led to an explosion of community-based consultation and research activities. At the same time there has been a recognition that if local programmes and projects are to be effective then they have to take account of local needs, local priorities and the views of local people. While not all of the community-based research activity undertaken by or for public agencies has conformed to the community development model advocated in this book there have, none the less, been some serious attempts to involve local people in the assessment of their own needs and to take account of their views in the design and delivery of local services.

Community and voluntary organizations have recognized the power of information in developing community campaigns and also in raising awareness of issues. The development of models of how to do community profiles – in both urban and rural contexts – has greatly facilitated this process.

At the same time the massive increase in the ease with which data and information can be accessed through the internet has also contributed to community profiling; basic statistics for most local areas can now be accessed online in relatively easy-to-use formats. Similarly, the media available to communicate and disseminate the findings of community profiles have developed, widening the opportunities for communities to get their message across more effectively. However, these developments have also had the potentially negative consequence of seeming to raise the bar for communities wanting to do their own research. Many of the community profiles now produced are very glossy and expertly put together, but community groups need to remember that while research rigour is important in making findings credible, and presentation can make a difference in how findings are received, as important is the telling quote from a community member, the demonstration of passion and commitment that informs a presentation of results and the evidence of local knowledge.

So it is a welcome development that community profiles are now positively encouraged – by both central government agencies and also local government – and increasingly easy to undertake. However, we should not lose sight of what has, traditionally, been the radical potential of community profiles – to bring about change by: highlighting poverty and disadvantage, and needs that are not being met; drawing attention to inequality in the allocation of resources; raising awareness of the impact on ordinary people of decisions taken by 'bigger players'; and enabling communities to develop understanding, skills, confidence and a sense of themselves as communities.

Appendix 1
Glossary

Action planning/action plan The process through which members of a community work together to produce a plan setting out their vision and priorities for their neighbourhood or community and the action which will help to achieve them.

Area profile Developed by the Audit Commission, area profiles bring together a wide range of local data to provide a profile of each local authority in England. An area profile includes demographic information together with data on the performance of services, assessments made by independent inspectorates and residents' views as indicated by local surveys (see www.areaprofiles.audit-commission.gov.uk).

Capacity building Input of resources, training and support to strengthen the skills, abilities and confidence of people and community groups to take effective action in and for their communities.

CAQDAS This stands for Computer Assisted Qualitative Data Analysis Software, but is often referred to as QDA software or qualitative software. It refers to a range of different software packages that have been produced to support qualitative research. They are of especial use in assisting the detailed exploration, coding and analysis of textual data. (See Chapter 8.)

Case study A case study focuses on one particular instance of a phenomenon (or case) in order to explore in depth a typical or atypical example.

Citizens' jury Made up of around 16 people selected as far as possible to reflect the community. The jury sits for three to five days and considers often controversial issues before reaching a 'verdict' in the form of a report on the issue. Presentations are heard from 'witnesses' who offer different points of view on the issue under consideration.

Citizens' panel Sometimes referred to as panel survey, a citizens' panel is an ongoing panel made up of a sample of local people who agree to complete a set number of surveys each year and/or volunteer to take part in other consultative processes. It functions as a sounding board and often focuses on specific services, policy issues or on wider strategy.

Closed question A question that permits only a limited range of responses such as 'yes' or 'no' and does not allow the respondent to elaborate in any way.

Coding The assigning of numerical values to non-numerical variables to facilitate analysis.

Community audit A community audit is very similar to a community profile, providing a comprehensive picture of a neighbourhood, to help shape its plans for the future.

Community consultation Typically initiated by a statutory body or other agency, a community consultation is usually designed to gauge the attitudes of the community towards a set of proposals, options or priorities or to assess satisfaction with an existing service.

Community development The process of collective action to achieve social justice and change by working with communities to identify needs and take action to meet them. It is based on an agreed set of values and is particularly important to vulnerable groups and disadvantaged communities.

Community involvement The involvement of people from a given locality or section of local population in public decision making and other local activities.

Community organization/group A community organization or group consists of people who combine together in pursuit of shared objectives in which they themselves have an interest. It differs from a voluntary organization in that the control lies in the hands of the beneficiaries as individual users, members or residents.

Community participation See *Community involvement*.

Community plan/strategy A comprehensive strategy for promoting the well-being of an area that aims to coordinate the actions of the key local organizations so that they effectively meet community needs and aspirations.

Community profile A comprehensive description of the needs of a population that is defined, or defines itself, as a community, and the resources that exist within that community, carried out with the active involvement of the community itself, for the purpose of developing an action plan or other means of improving the quality of life of the community.

Cross-tabulation Often referred to as a cross-tab, this is a research tool used in quantitative analysis to analyse differences across sub-groups in a sample population. It is a way of organizing frequencies (often in a table) showing the relationship between two or more nominal variables. A cross-tabulation table contains individual cells, with the number in each cell representing the frequency of participants who show that particular combination of characteristics.

Data analysis This is the process of studying and transforming raw data so that its meaning, structure, relationships, origins, etc. are understood and it becomes usable.

Faith community A faith community is a community of people adhering to the same religion or belief system. Faith communities can be viewed as a distinctive part of the voluntary and community sector and within a faith community there may be faith groups that effectively operate as voluntary or community organizations.

Focus group A common type of group discussion or interview with a selected group of individuals (usually eight to ten people). A moderator or enabler encourages the group to focus gradually on a particular topic with the aim of obtaining their views and experiences on that topic. Focus groups are particularly useful for obtaining a range of perspectives about a topic, as well as exploring ideas.

Frequency/frequency distribution A measure of the rate at which something happens or is repeated. It describes how cases are distributed over different data values on a particular variable. A frequency table, therefore, will give you an overview of the number (or percentage) of respondents who gave each answer to a question.

Local Strategic Partnership (LSP) An LSP is a multi-agency body which works within local authority boundaries to bring together key local organizations from the public, private, community and voluntary sectors.

Needs assessment This will tend to be initiated and/or carried out by a statutory agency, for example a Primary Care Trust or local authority department, for policy planning purposes. Needs assessments generally make use of existing data (for example, population data), although this may be supplemented with additional sources that provide intelligence on attitudes to, and perceptions of, local needs on the part of those most likely to be affected by a service.

Observation Observation as a research method can be carried out in a variety of situations including 'natural' settings such as a shop or a bus. The observer may be a participant, e.g. a member of the committee that s/he is observing, or 'concealed' (in other words, the fact that s/he is observing is not disclosed). Observation can take place in a structured way, involving a specific list of things that are being looked for, or unstructured, involving the observer writing down everything that s/he sees. Observation can be useful in finding out about people's actions and behaviour and the way in which they interact with each other and the physical environment.

Open question A question that requires respondents to elaborate on what they think rather than giving a simple factual or 'yes/no' response.

Oral testimony/history Oral testimony or history is the study of an area, a group of people or a community using the recollections and experiences of people who have lived in the area or experienced the events under study. The data is usually collected using in-depth interviews, often recorded on tape.

Output area In the 2001 census output areas replaced enumeration districts. Each output area contains around 125 households. The output areas then 'nest' within wards and parishes. Output areas have also been grouped to form super output areas (SOAs), which are widely used to present key data from the census.

Parish appraisal see *Village appraisal.*

Participant observation See *Observation.*

Participatory approach Participatory research refers less to the specific methods employed and more to the general approach used. A participatory approach is one in which those people who might otherwise be the *subjects* of research become active participants in the process. Participatory research methods are often used in a community development context as a means of empowering local people and developing their skills and confidence. More traditional research methods can often be adapted to make them more participatory. For example, a community profile can be designed and overseen by local residents; members of the local community can determine the research questions; use can be made of local knowledge of history and issues relating to the neighbourhood; local people can be employed as interviewers; and residents can participate in the analysis and interpretation of data.

Piloting Trying out your research approach and any research instruments with a small number of people in order to check that they work in the way that you expect them to.

Planning for Real Developed by the Neighbourhood Initiatives Foundation, this technique results in the construction of a large 3D model of the neighbourhood which is then used by local people to demonstrate their needs and ideas for future development.

Practitioner research Research carried out by practitioners to inform the development of their own professional practice. Practitioner research may take the form of needs analysis, evaluations or service reviews.

Primary data See *Primary research.*

Primary research The collection, analysis and interpretation of new information.

Qualitative methods Generate data that cannot usually be presented numerically. Qualitative methods are useful for in-depth understanding of issues and for providing information about attitudes, perceptions and feelings.

Quantitative methods Produce data that measures things numerically and that can be aggregated (added up).

Reliability Research results are reliable if there is a reasonable expectation that if someone else undertook the same investigation they would obtain similar results.

Response rate The proportion of those receiving a questionnaire who return it.

Response sample Those returning a completed questionnaire or responding to an invitation to participate in interviews.

Secondary data Data that is already in existence, that has been collected by someone else but that can be used for your own purposes.

Semi-structured interview Conversational open discussion using a checklist of questions as a flexible guide instead of a formal questionnaire.

Social accounting See *Social auditing.*

Social auditing A regular cyclical process through which an organization's performance is assessed in relation to its own objectives and those of wider stakeholder groups. The process involves extensive dialogue with stakeholders and external verification.

Social capital Local networks, together with shared norms, values and under-standings that facilitate cooperation within or between groups.

Social exclusion This is what can happen when a combination of linked prob-lems such as unemployment, lack of skills, low incomes, discrimination, poor housing, high levels of crime, poor health and family breakdown lead to people or places being excluded from the outcomes and opportun-ities enjoyed by mainstream society.

Structured interview/questionnaire An interview or questionnaire that requires the interviewer or respondent to work through a series of ques-tions in which the wording is closely specified.

Super output area see *Output area.*

Survey A social survey is a method of obtaining often large amounts of data from a large number of people in a relatively short space of time. This data is often presented in statistical form. Social surveys may be undertaken through face-to-face interviews, telephone interviews, by email or through a self-completion questionnaire. In all cases surveys use a standardized set of questions which may be 'closed' or 'open'. With closed questions the survey respondent typically selects a category from a prescribed list of possible answers. With open questions the respondent answers the ques-tion in his or her own way. Closed questions make it easy for the researcher to organize the responses into categories and quantify them. However, they may make it difficult to get more than a superficial under-standing of issues. Open questions allow respondents to express their own views but make it difficult for the researcher to organize or quantify the responses. Many survey questionnaires use a mixture of open and closed questions.

Valid (data) Valid data measures what it purports to measure.

Village appraisal A village or parish appraisal is a means of rural communities identifying local characteristics, problems, needs and issues as part of the process of rural development. In many ways they are the rural equivalent of predominantly urban community profiles. While there is no blueprint for undertaking a parish appraisal, most reflect a similar set of general principles and make use of a local survey.

Voluntary organization A group whose activities are carried out other than for profit but which are not public or local authorities. These organizations are normally formally constituted and employ paid professional and administrative staff.

Appendix 2
Further information on social research methods

In the main part of the book we have, wherever possible, left out any discussion of the more technical aspects of social research methods in order to avoid cluttering up the text with information that would be of limited interest to many readers. This appendix is intended to provide a very basic guide to the more technical aspects of social research methods of relevance to community profiling. In particular this appendix should provide you with sufficient information to carry out a survey successfully. It covers the following topics:

- sampling;
- questionnaire development;
- distribution and collection of questionnaires;
- recruitment and training of interviewers;
- using statistics.

Sampling

When considering what kind of survey method to adopt, you will need to give some thought to your sample. The sample is the group of people who are directly involved in the survey through being interviewed or sent a self-completion questionnaire. Sampling can be quite a difficult technical exercise but it is important, since it can affect the validity and reliability of the information that you collect (see Chapters 7 and 9). If your sample is not appropriate then you might end up with information that is not very useful. Again, it is worth seeking assistance from others with particular expertise in this area, although this section should provide you with the basic knowledge to derive a sample.

In thinking about your sample, your starting point will be the whole community in which you are interested. Having drawn an imaginary line around this community, you must then decide on the kinds of people within the community from whom you are interested in obtaining information. Let's take as an example a spatially defined community such as a housing estate. Are you interested only in the views of those who live on the estate or those who are employed there as well? Are you interested in everyone's views or only those of the adult residents? Are you taking 18 or 16 as the age at which people are deemed to be adults?

Having answered these questions and decided on the type of people whose views interest you, you must then decide how many people you can reasonably contact given the survey methods you intend to use, the resources you have at your disposal and the timescale for completion of the project. Whether you have access to a computer to store and analyse the information that you collect may be an important consideration in deciding how many people to survey (see Chapter 8).

Of course, it may be the case that you want to ask questions of everyone within a particular group of people, for example all the adult residents of an estate. If so, then you have what is called a 100 per cent sample and you have no need to go any further through the process of deriving a sample. In most cases, unless your community is quite small or your resources quite large, this will not be practical and you will need to find a smaller group of people to survey. In deciding who this sample of people should consist of, you need to bear in mind two issues: the number of people you want to contact and how representative this group is of the community as a whole. What it means for a sample to be representative is that the characteristics of your sample match as closely as possible those of the community at large. The characteristics which are generally considered to be important are gender, age, ethnicity, place of residence and employment status. However, depending on the purpose of your profile, there may be other characteristics that are also important. So, if you know that 25 per cent of the population is aged over 65 in your community, then you should try to ensure that your sample contains 25 per cent of people over 65. If you end up with responses from a larger proportion of people over 65, then it is possible that the views expressed will be biased and fail to reflect accurately the views of the wider community. In order to ensure that your sample is representative, you will need some information about the characteristics of the population that makes up the community in which you are interested, which you can then use to work out how many of each group you should try to have in your sample. In most cases, this can be obtained from census data (see Chapter 6).

Sampling frames

Having decided on the population to be sampled, identified the characteristics of that population and decided how many individuals from each group you want in your sample, you must then obtain a sampling frame. A sampling frame is essentially a comprehensive list of those individuals or organizations relevant to your survey from which you will derive the actual individuals or organizations who will be contacted. It might be the electoral register for a particular area, a list of voluntary or community organizations, a list of ward councillors or a register of users of a particular service. You need to be sure that your sampling frame includes all the people that interest you. For example, if you want to include 16-year-olds in your sample, then the electoral register will not be much use because only those aged 17 and above are included. Also, you must be sure that you have excluded from the sampling frame all those who are not relevant. For example, if you are only interested in surveying women, then you must make sure that your sampling frame contains only women. If your sampling frame does not allow you to identify the particular characteristics of individuals in which you are interested, then you may need to identify a larger initial sample and then use some kind of screening mechanism for excluding those who do not fit your criteria (see below).

The electoral register is one of the most widely used sampling frames. The electoral registration office of your local authority will have a register of the names and addresses of all those aged 17 and over who have registered to vote. The register is organized by polling district and street, so it is quite easy to find the streets that relate to the area you want to profile. However, there are a number of disadvantages associated with drawing your sample from the electoral register. First, not all those who live in the area will have registered to vote and, indeed, it may be the case that those who are most needy or vulnerable are precisely those who have not registered. Furthermore, the electoral register will not tell you whether people are black or white, employed or unemployed, young or old, so if you want to focus on a particular group in the population then this is a problem. Nevertheless, despite difficulties, it may prove to be the most comprehensive list of adults available.

Having obtained a comprehensive sampling frame, you must now decide on the technique for drawing your sample that is most appropriate to your project. There are three main approaches: random sampling, stratified sampling and quota sampling.

Random sampling

Random sampling is so called because everyone included in the sampling frame has an equal chance of being selected. However, random in this context does not mean haphazard. For example, it would not be a random sample if you simply walked down a street interviewing everyone you happened to encounter. Some residents would be at home or at work or somewhere else and so could not be said to have had an equal chance of being interviewed. Random sampling is a technique with rules that must be adhered to. Nevertheless, it is a fairly simple technique. You can derive a random sample in two ways. The first is to use a set of random number tables which can usually be found at the back of statistics textbooks, or you can buy books of random numbers, or you can use a computer to generate a random number. Random numbers usually appear as five digits and, reading from the left, you should use as many of the digits as you need in order to identify your sample. So, if there are fewer than 100 individuals in your sampling frame, use only the first two digits of each random number. If there are between 100 and 999 individuals, use three digits and so on. Simply work through the lists of random numbers either going down the column or up the column or from left to right or right to left, but always consistently. Once you have a set of random numbers equivalent to the number you want to arrive at in your sample, then you can identify the sample by picking out the numbers of those individuals in the sampling frame to match the random numbers.

An easier way to obtain a random sample is to take the number of individuals in the sampling frame and divide it by the number of people you want to end up with in your sample in order to obtain the sampling interval. Then, using a random number that is less than the total number of individuals in the sampling frame, use the individual in the sampling frame who corresponds to that number as your starting point and use the sampling interval to identify the next name, and so on. So if you have a sampling frame of 2000 and you want a sample of 200, then you will have a sampling interval of 10. If the random number tables give you a number of 596, then the individual who appears as 596th on the list will be the first in the sample. Working from here you should then identify every tenth entry on the list, going back to the beginning when you reach the last entry, until you have your sample of 200. This method of sampling is very easy to do but cannot be used if there is a bias of any kind in the sampling frame. In other words, if the list groups people in any way, for example by age, then this kind of sampling cannot be used.

Stratified random sampling

An alternative, slightly more complex approach is to use stratified random sampling. This technique is particularly useful when you want to guarantee that certain sections of the community are included. So, for example, if you have a community that consists of three identifiably different populations, for example a white population, a Pakistani population and an African-Caribbean population, you may want to stratify your sample so that it is proportional to these three constituent elements. So if the total population is 5000 and 3000 of these people (or 60 per cent) are white and 1000 (or 20 per cent) are Pakistani and a further 1000 (or 20 per cent) African-Caribbean, you would need to ensure that the sample contained appropriate proportions of these three groups. In practice, you would need separate sampling frames for each of the three communities and then randomly sample the appropriate number of individuals from each as described above.

Quota sampling

A third method of sampling is quota sampling. This is similar in some respects to stratified sampling in that the aim is to ensure that the sample reflects certain known characteristics of the population; for example, if you know that 25 per cent of the population is aged over 65, then 25 per cent of the people in your sample should also be over 65. However, quota samples are usually based on more than one characteristic. For example, you may want to take account of gender, age, ethnicity and employment status. The sample that you derive should then ensure that it contains appropriate proportions of people with these characteristics. The important difference here is that the sample is not derived entirely randomly. Rather, the researcher sets out to find appropriate numbers of people with the particular characteristics specified in the quota.

Cluster sampling

There is one other kind of sampling technique, cluster sampling, which may be important if you are dealing with a community that is widely dispersed, for example women in a particular city or district. This technique actually involves two layers of sampling: the first samples areas of the city or district and the second identifies individuals within those areas. Thus the sample is clustered in that individuals identified in the sample are concentrated in particular parts of the city. This is especially useful when it is not practicable for interviewers to cover a very large geographical area or where it would be too costly or time-consuming to work through a very large sampling frame, for example the entire electoral register for a city.

The first thing to do is to divide the city or district into appropriate areas which can then be sampled. Usually, the easiest way to do this is on the basis of polling districts, census output areas or wards. First, you will need to know the total population for each area. List each area with the cumulative population next to it. Having decided how many areas you want to end up with, divide the total population for all the areas by the number of areas you want in the sample to give the sampling frame. Then, using a random number start, identify the areas by adding the sampling interval and then identifying the area which contains the cumulative population total that contains this figure. The reason for doing this is that no matter whether areas have large or small populations, they have an equal chance of being sampled. Alternatively, you may want to ensure that you include a range of different areas within a city or district which display certain characteristics. For example, you may want to ensure that you include rich and poor areas, white and multicultural, areas of owner-occupied housing and council estates. If so, you will need to specify the characteristics precisely, determine which indicators to use, group the areas appropriately and then randomly sample within these groupings. In effect, you are stratifying your sampling points using this method. Having identified the areas or sampling points, it is then possible to identify the sample of individuals using any of the methods described above.

Whichever method you decide to use to derive your sample, you should follow the rules carefully to ensure that the sample that you end up with is as unbiased as possible.

Questionnaire development

Wording questions

The wording of questions is very important. If you ask a question using inappropriate words, then the respondent may not understand what you are asking and will therefore be unable to answer the question. Or, if the question is asked insensitively, then he or she may refuse to answer. In general, the words used and the style in which questions are asked should be familiar to members of the community who will be responding to the questions and comfortable for interviewers to use. It is helpful to pilot your questionnaire in order to uncover potential difficulties.

There are a number of things to avoid at all costs. These will be discussed briefly in turn.

Leading questions
These questions encourage the respondent to answer in a particular way. An example of a leading question might be:

> *Don't you think this is a friendly neighbourhood?*

A better way of asking about a respondent's assessment of the friendliness of his or her neighbourhood might be as follows:

> *Please could you tell me how friendly you think this neighbourhood is?*
> *(Circle one)*
> *Very friendly   Fairly friendly   Not very friendly   Not at all friendly*

Vague questions
These questions include words that are open to different interpretations. An example might be as follows:

Do you often go to the cinema? (Tick one)
Yes ☐
No ☐

This is likely to lead to meaningless responses, since what counts as 'often' will vary enormously between individuals. A better way of asking this question might be as follows:

How often do you go to the cinema? (Tick one)
Never ☐
At least once a year ☐
At least once every six months ☐
At least once every three months ☐
. . . etc.

Ambiguous terms

Some commonly used words are too ambiguous to be used without definition. These include: unemployed, housewife, old people, young people, rich, poor, and so on. All of these terms will mean different things to different people. In general, it is best to avoid these terms altogether and use more precise words and phrases such as:

- not currently in paid work for 'unemployed';
- not in paid work and looking after home and family for 'housewife';
- aged 65 or over for 'old people';
- aged 16–21 for 'young people'.

Hypothetical questions

These are questions which ask people what they might do in certain hypothetical situations. An example might be:

If you were to move house where do you think you would move to?

This type of question is likely to elicit a lot of 'I don't know' responses, since many of those answering the question will not be interested in moving house and will therefore never have given the matter any thought at all. There may, however, be times when it is appropriate to use a hypothetical question, for example if you want to get people to express an ideal or a set of values. You might want to find out what is currently lacking in people's lives by asking a question like:

If you won £1000 what would you spend it on?

Two questions in one

These questions are worded in such a way that you are actually asking about two possibly unrelated issues at the same time. For example:

> *Do you think that there should be more car parking places or that people should walk to work?*

This question is almost impossible to answer as it asks two quite separate questions at the same time.

Questions that are too general

For example, a question such as:

> *What do you think about the houses in this area?*

This is very difficult to answer. Are you trying to find out about the state of repair of houses, their size, whether they are well designed, attractive to look at or comfortable to live in? It is far better to ask several more specific questions such as:

- *Do you think that the houses in this area are in a good state of repair?*
- *Would you say that the houses in this area are well designed?*
  . . . etc.

Questions which ask too much

An example of this type of question might be:

> *Please tell me about your last five visits to the doctor, why you went, how easy it was to get an appointment and what was the outcome of your visit?*

Far too much information is being sought in one question. Again, it is far better to ask about each issue in a separate question.

Questions which assume knowledge

This problem might arise where the language used is technical, or where jargon is included or where abbreviations are used. For example:

- *Does your home have uPVC windows?*
- *Do you think you have become institutionalized as a result of your long stay in hospital?*
- *How useful do you think NVQs are in finding a job?*

Unless you are certain that the people in your sample will understand this kind of technical language or jargon, then avoid using it.

Mental arithmetic questions

It is not a good idea to ask people to do arithmetical calculations, whether it is a self-completion questionnaire or an interview. For example:

> *Please could you tell me what your total weekly household income is from all sources including wages or salary, benefits of all kinds and pensions.*

In this case, it would be far better and result in a higher degree of accuracy to list all the possible sources of income and go through them individually and for the interviewer or coder to do the adding up.

Questions that rely on a good memory

It is unlikely that you will get very accurate responses if you ask people about events too far in the past. For example:

> *How many times did you go to the local swimming pool over the last year?*

In general, the previous six months is a reasonable timescale about which to ask questions. However, where possible ask about a shorter and more recent time period and, where appropriate, fix it in people's minds by reference to an event such as Christmas.

Piloting the questionnaire

Once you have drafted the questionnaire, you need to test that it actually works. The best way to do this is to try it out on a small group of people who have not been involved in the drafting. This will help you to find out whether the questions can be understood and answered appropriately; whether the filter questions work properly; whether the possible answers to your closed questions are sufficiently comprehensive; whether there is enough space to record the answers and so on. During the piloting, the questionnaire should be used in the same way that it will be used in the actual survey. So, if it is to be a self-completion questionnaire, then it should be given to those participating in the pilot with no additional information besides the covering letter which would normally accompany the questionnaire (see p. 140). If it is to be an interview, then the interviewer should introduce the questionnaire in the same way that it will be introduced in the survey proper.

Once the pilot questionnaires have been completed, you need to look at the responses and talk to those involved in the pilot – respondents and interviewers – and ask the following questions.

- Are the types of responses to the questions broadly what you expected?
- Can the responses be coded?

- Where some parts of the questionnaire or some questions only apply to certain groups of respondents, do the filtering questions work properly?
- Do any questions seem to have been consistently misinterpreted?
- Do any questions seem redundant?
- Were any questions difficult to ask or to answer?
- Did questions involving show cards work okay?
- Did any of the categories in pre-coded questions seem redundant?
- Did a lot of closed questions elicit responses that fell in to the 'other' category?
- How long did it take to complete the questionnaire?

Having carried out the pilot and addressed the issues identified in the review, you should now be in a position to produce the final draft of your questionnaire. Once any amendments arising out of the pilot have been incorporated, it will need to be proofread and the numbering checked (especially where questions have been reordered or taken out or added). Survey questionnaires should always be typed or word-processed. Now it is ready to be printed or photocopied.

Distribution and return of self-completion questionnaires

If your survey is of the self-completion type, you will have to arrange for the questionnaires to be delivered to the people identified in your sample. Essentially, there are three ways to do this: post them, deliver them by hand or personally give them to the individuals concerned. Whichever method you choose to employ, you must be certain that you know who the questionnaires have been delivered to and which of them has been returned to you. You must also check that when the questionnaires are delivered to the sample they know what they are supposed to do with them and why they have received them.

If the questionnaires are delivered by post or by hand, then they will need to be clearly addressed to the person who is to complete them. Where you do not have a named individual to send the questionnaire to, then you will have to address it to 'The Occupier' or 'The Resident'. You will then need to state clearly in the covering letter and on the questionnaire itself who within the household is to complete the questionnaire. Whatever method is used to deliver the questionnaire it should be accompanied by a letter or leaflet explaining what the survey is about, how to complete the questionnaire, what to do with it when it is completed and what will happen next. The accompanying letter or leaflet should also give an assurance of confidentiality.

If you want respondents to return their questionnaires to you by post, then you will have to include a pre-paid, addressed envelope of an appropriate size when the questionnaire is sent out. Alternatively, you may want to increase the response rate by calling on people and asking them to give you their completed questionnaire or, if they have not yet completed it, ask them if they require any help to do so. This is especially useful in areas where you suspect that poor literacy may affect the response. If you decide to use this method of returning the questionnaires, then you should make it clear in the covering letter accompanying the questionnaire that someone will be calling on them, and indicate the approximate timescale between delivery and collection of the questionnaire. You should still include an envelope with the questionnaire, as some people may feel uncomfortable handing you a form which contains personal information about themselves or their household, especially where those collecting the questionnaires are local volunteers. Of course, you may decide to use pre-paid envelopes for the bulk of responses and only call on those who have not responded within a certain time. This has the advantage of maximizing the amount of time available for chasing up those who might otherwise not respond. If you want to do the whole survey entirely by post, you may instead want to send a reminder letter to those who have not returned their questionnaire to you within a specified time.

Another method of returning questionnaires is to get people to hand them in to a particular place, for example a community centre. However, this is the most demanding way of getting questionnaires returned, since it requires the most effort on the part of the respondent. As a consequence, it may result in a lower response rate than would otherwise be the case.

Logging responses

Whichever method you decide to use to get the questionnaires back, you will need to be able to keep a record of which ones have been returned. This is especially important if you are intending to follow up non-respondents. The simplest way to do this is to give each person or household in your sample an identification number which is written on the questionnaire and also against the name and address of the individual concerned. As questionnaires are returned, you can then simply tick them off so that those who have not yet responded can easily be identified. If you are using a computer to log responses, it is very important that the file containing the names and addresses of individuals in your sample is separate from the data relating to them.

You may also want to keep an eye on response rates from particular groups within your overall sample, so that you can identify especially low responses in certain quarters at an early stage and take appropriate action (e.g. reminder letters, visits) to boost the response from such groups. If you are going to do this, then you will need to have some basic information on the characteristics of the population (see above) to enable you to assess whether response rates are particularly low or high.

Recruitment and training of interviewers

If you are undertaking an interview survey, then you will have to recruit and train the interviewers. This will apply whether the interviewers are to be paid or are unpaid volunteers (see Chapter 4). Before you begin the process of recruitment, you will need to decide how many interviewers you need. This will vary depending on the size of the community you are profiling and the length of time you have available to do the work. In general, it is probably better to have as few interviewers as possible unless you are using local volunteers and the profiling exercise is being used to develop local people's skills, confidence and awareness (see Chapter 4). From a practical point of view, it is easier to manage the process and ensure consistency if relatively few people are involved. If you have sufficient people within the group involved in the profiling exercise with the necessary time and skills, then you will be able to avoid the lengthy task of recruitment described below. However, you should be careful that the interviewers, if they are drawn from the project group, are not seen by the community as an exclusive clique.

Recruitment

Whether your interviewers are going to be paid or not, you will probably want to recruit people who are part of the community to be profiled or have some knowledge of it. This means that you can probably restrict advertisements to the locality in the case of a geographically located community or to places or papers that are targeted at a particular group in the case of a community of interest. Any advertisement, whether it is a notice in a community centre or in the 'situations vacant' column of your local newspaper, needs to give the title of the project, what is entailed in the job (e.g. interviewing people in their own homes), how many hours, days and weeks of work are required, what skills or expertise you are looking for (e.g. sensitivity, knowledge of an ethnic minority language) and, if appropriate, what the rate of pay will be. Don't forget to include a contact point for further information, details of how people should go about applying for the job and the deadline for applications.

One way of recruiting interviewers is to advertise an open recruitment session at an appropriate venue or venues and invite interested people to come and talk about the project at a particular time. If you are going to use this method, you will need to make sure that you have enough people from the steering group or management group available to assist with interviewing and that you are there throughout the day and evening so that people in different circumstances can attend. It is a good idea to ask people to complete a simple application form in order to get basic information, such as name, address, telephone number, any relevant experience, availability for work and so on.

You should also ask for the names and addresses of two referees. If you are sending people out to talk to people in their own homes, then it is only fair that you have taken some steps to establish that they are of good character.

Once applicants have completed their application forms, you could then interview them to assess their suitability. This is best done with two people interviewing each candidate. If you are expecting a lot of candidates you may want to devise a simple form that can be used by the interviewers to record their impressions of the candidates and their suitability for the work. It goes without saying that the basic principles of equal opportunities procedures should apply, namely that you should only take into account relevant characteristics, qualifications and experience.

Once you have selected your interviewers, you should write to them confirming that they have been appointed and setting out the terms of the job. Your letter should make it clear that they are required to attend a training session on a particular day and that they should bring with them a passport-sized photograph to that session to be used on their identification card.

Training

The training of interviewers, whether paid or unpaid, is vital if the survey is to be successful. You will need to find a room large enough to accommodate comfortably the group of interviewers and trainers, and to devise a programme for the training day or days. During the course of the training you should cover the following issues:

- what the survey is about;
- who is organizing the survey;
- familiarization with survey materials;
- setting up interviews;
- working with quotas;
- introductions;
- interviewing techniques;
- confidentiality;
- recording responses;
- personal security;
- dealing with difficult situations;
- finishing the interview;
- survey administration;
- quality controls and back-checking.

These will be discussed briefly in turn. Most of what follows relates particularly to surveys involving face-to-face, structured interviews with people in their own homes. However, some will also be of relevance to other kinds of

interview surveys. At the end of this section, we include some issues of particular relevance to street interviewing, telephone interviewing, semi-structured
interviews and group discussions.

What is the survey about?

It is important that the interviewers understand why the survey is taking place,
what kind of information is to be collected and why, and what will happen to
the information once it has been collated and analysed. The better their
understanding of the survey, the more committed they are likely to be and the
better will be the quality of the information that they collect; if the interviewers know what you are interested in, they are more likely to be able to record
this information accurately. Also, it is important that the interviewers can
confidently answer the questions of those they are seeking to interview about
the nature and purpose of the survey.

Who is organizing the survey?

Interviewers need to know exactly who is organizing the survey and be able to
answer questions about this from potential interviewees who may be highly
suspicious of someone appearing on their doorstep armed with a clipboard.

Familiarization with survey materials

The more familiar interviewers are with the survey questionnaire or interview
schedule, the more confident they will be in the interview and the more accurate will be the information that you will obtain. It is a good idea to go through
the questionnaire explaining what information each question is seeking and
how any filter questions work, giving examples of responses and inviting questions. Once you have done this, you should allow as much time as possible for
the interviewers to practise using the questionnaire with each other. One way
of doing this is to work through the questionnaire with all the interviewers in a
group taking it in turns to ask each consecutive question. You may then want
to allow time for them to work in pairs taking it in turns to role-play
interviewees.

Setting up interviews

The interviewers will need to understand fully how they are to find people to
interview. This will depend on the kind of sample you are using. In most cases,
the interviewers will be given a list of addresses to call on, or named individuals within identifiable households or the names of streets with an instruction to call at every 'nth' house. Whichever method you use, make sure that
the interviewers have appropriate written instructions to which they can
refer. The interviewers also need instructions on when to call on potential
interviewees and how often they should call back if interviewees are not at
home. A common method of working is to suggest that people do not begin

interviewing before ten o'clock in the morning and should not work past nine o'clock at night, and that you should allow up to three visits on different days and at different times of the day to try to catch people at home. Any calls to a particular address should be recorded either on the front of the interview schedule or on a separate record sheet.

Working with quotas
If you are using a system of quotas, the interviewers will need details of how the quota system works and how to keep records (see the section on quota sampling on p. 135).

Introductions
How interviewers introduce themselves to potential interviewees is likely to influence whether or not the interviewee agrees to be interviewed. It is a good idea to get each interviewer to come up with a form of words with which they feel comfortable. This should explain who they are, who they are working for and the fact that they would like to interview the person concerned. Where a named individual is being sought within the household or a quota sample is being used, then they also need to find appropriate words to check that they are talking to the right person. The following list summarizes the key points of relevance to introductions.

- Say who you are and what organization you are from.
- Show your identification card and invite the interviewee to check it.
- Tell the interviewee about the survey. It might be helpful to show him or her a copy of a publicity leaflet as a memory jogger, if one has been produced.
- Check who you are speaking to and invite her or him to be interviewed if this is the right person, or ask to speak to someone else in the household if not.
- Be prepared to answer any questions that might be asked. How long will it take? How did you get hold of my name? What will happen to the information?
- Give an assurance of confidentiality.
- If the person appears reluctant to be interviewed, try to find out why and give answers to their objections – but accept that anyone has the right to refuse to participate.
- Be friendly, confident and enthusiastic about the survey.

Interviewing techniques
The interviewers will need some basic training in interviewing techniques. Much of this is common sense and will come naturally to anyone with good listening skills. However, there are some issues which ought to be emphasized.

These include: the importance of reading the question exactly as it appears in the questionnaire; not prompting the respondent except where there is a specific instruction to 'probe'; showing that they are listening to the respondent by nodding and smiling; remaining neutral with regard to the content of the questions and the answers (neither agreeing nor disagreeing); and not getting drawn in to arguments or discussions with the interviewee.

Confidentiality

The importance of confidentiality should be stressed throughout the training. The interviewers must understand the importance of not discussing the content of interviews with others and of keeping all completed interview schedules in a secure place. Arrangements should be made for the interviewers to return completed questionnaires to the survey organizers as soon as possible after completion.

Recording responses

The interviewers should practise recording responses to questions during their training. They need to understand the importance of working through the questionnaire systematically, carefully following any instructions. All responses should be recorded accurately and honestly. If interviewers are unsure of how to record a response or which category to put it in, they should be instructed to make a note on the form detailing the precise answer and then to check with the survey organizer precisely how the answer should be recorded. The general rule should be that if they are in any doubt, they should write down more rather than less information. This is especially the case with open-ended questions. For pre-coded questions, the appropriate box should be ticked or the appropriate response circled clearly. If an interviewer makes a mistake or a respondent changes his or her mind, it is important that the intended response is clearly identified.

If the respondent answers 'none' to a question, then this should be written on the form. Leaving a blank or putting a dash might give the impression that the question was not asked, or the respondent refused to answer. All responses should be written clearly, especially when someone else has responsibility for coding, inputting and analysing the information.

After the interview has been completed, the interviewer should check through the form to make sure that all responses are legible and that no questions have been missed. It is a good idea for the interviewers to be encouraged to make comments about the process, for example difficulties with the interview itself, problems in using the questionnaire and so on.

Personal security

All interviewers should be fully briefed on personal security. This briefing should stress the importance of carrying their identification card with them at all times. This card should have a picture of the interviewer, his or her name and the name of the organization carrying out the survey, and it should be signed by a representative of that organization. It should also have a telephone number which interviewees can ring in order to verify the identity of the interviewer. The interviewers should also have written down an emergency telephone number which they can ring if they have a problem. It is a good idea to inform the local police station in writing that a survey is being conducted in a particular area, giving them the dates, the names of the interviewers and their car registrations where appropriate. It is usually best to send interviewers out to work particular streets or areas in pairs with an instruction that they contact the survey organizers if one of them has not seen the other for a while. Depending on the areas in which they are working, it can sometimes be helpful to equip interviewers with personal alarms and hand-held dog dazers (ultrasonic dog deterrence aids).

In general, personal security relies on the good sense of the interviewers, although the above precautions will help protect them while they are out in the field. The basic rule should be that interviewers should take appropriate steps to minimize risk and should back off from any situation in which they feel uncomfortable, even if this means terminating an interview prematurely. One way of doing this is for interviewers to look at their watch and say they have to check back with a colleague.

Survey organizers have a duty to take appropriate steps to protect not only their interviewers but also those being interviewed. This means that interviewers should be trustworthy and provided with character references from appropriate referees. You may also want to think carefully about what kind of interviewer you employ for particular projects.

Dealing with difficult situations

The interviewers need to be given advice during their training about dealing with difficult or potentially difficult situations. Interviewing people about issues that are important to them can arouse strong feelings of anger or distress. The interviewers need to have some idea of what to do in these situations. Again, common sense and sensitivity will cover most situations. However, it is a good idea to remind the interviewers that it is not their job to engage with the emotions of those they are interviewing or to offer counselling or advice. If an interviewee is clearly upset or angered by a particular question, the interviewer might gently suggest that they move on to the next one or suggest that they terminate the interview. The interviewers should never promise interviewees that they will take action on their behalf.

Finishing the interview

When the interviewer has worked through the questionnaire, the interviewee should be given the opportunity to make any general comments about the content of the survey and on the way it has been carried out. It is also a good idea to leave them with a leaflet which thanks them for taking part and informs them what will happen next.

Survey administration

The interviewers need to be provided with the basic tools which are required to undertake the interviews. This will include:

- pens and pencils;
- clipboard;
- blank questionnaires;
- paper;
- map of the area;
- contact names of key local people;
- emergency phone numbers;
- identification card;
- quota instructions;
- list of names and/or addresses;
- publicity leaflets about the survey;
- thank you leaflets.

They also need to know where to go to get new interview schedules and further names and addresses, and where and how often they should return completed questionnaires. If the interviewers are to be paid, you will also need to deal with issues relating to pay, expenses and national insurance.

Quality controls and back-checking

All completed questionnaires need to be checked for accuracy and to make sure that they contain no ambiguities (see also the section on coding and editing in Chapter 8). You may also want to do back-checking. This means that the survey organizer contacts a sample of those interviewed to check that the interviewer did call on them at the time stated on the form, that the interview was conducted in a satisfactory manner and that certain basic items of information (especially those pertaining to quotas) have been recorded accurately.

Basic statistics

When producing a community profile it is hard to avoid working with some statistics. Statistics are essentially a numerical way of representing information. There are three main kinds of statistics that you will need to know about: frequencies, averages and cross-tabulations.

Frequencies

Frequencies describe the number of times a particular value occurs in the data set. Frequencies may be expressed as whole numbers or percentages. So, for example, gender is a variable with two values – that is, male and female. If your data set contains responses from 200 people of whom 120 (or 60 per cent) are women and 80 (or 40 per cent) are men, then this is the frequency for the variable 'gender'.

Averages

There are three ways of expressing an average: mode, median or mean. Which one you use will depend on the type of variable and the way in which the information was stored. For example, if we take a variable such as age of respondents, the frequency distribution might be as shown in Figure A2.1.

Figure A2.1 Age distribution (notional)

Age of respondents (years)	Number	Percentage
21	3	6
25	7	2
29	6	12
34	10	20
38	5	10
42	6	12
47	2	4
54	3	6
63	1	2
68	3	6
75	4	8
Total	50	100

To work out the average age of respondents, it is necessary to add together the ages of all respondents (2017) and divide by the number of respondents (50) to give a mean age of 40.3 years. If, however, the ages of respondents were stored in bands (e.g. 20–29, 30–39, 40–49, 50–59, 60–69, and 70 and over) it would not be possible to compute the mean age. In this case, it would be better to use either the median or mode. The median is the middle place on a ranking scale. In the example in Figure A2.2 (overleaf), the median length of time that respondents have lived at their current address is 1–5 years, as this is the category which includes the 50 per cent mark. In this example, the median is also the mode. The mode is the single most common response. In this case, 15 out of 50 lived at their current address for 1–5 years, which is the single largest response category.

Figure A2.2   Length of time at current address

Years	Number	Percentage	Cumulative percentage
<1	13	26	26
1–5	15	30	56
6–10	8	16	72
11–15	6	12	84
15–20	3	6	90
>20	5	10	100

Cross-tabulation

So far we have looked only at a single variable. However, you will almost certainly want to look at the relationship between two or more variables. For example, we might want to look at the relationship between gender and the wish to see more services provided in the area, as in the example in Figure A2.3.

Figure A2.3   Gender X wish to see additional services

	More services (%)	No more services (%)
Men	33.4	66.6
Women	76.9	23.1

This is a cross-tabulation of two variables and it indicates that there may be a relationship between the gender of respondents and their response to this particular question, which allows us to say that women are more likely to express a desire for additional services. This is important for two reasons. First, it might suggest further lines of enquiry such as finding out (perhaps using one of the other methods suggested in Chapter 7) exactly what services women feel are lacking, or interrogating the data set further to see if it can tell us anything else about this issue, for example the age of women seeking additional services, whether or not they have children and whether or not they are in employment. This might involve looking at three variables simultaneously, for example gender, desire for additional services and employment status. It can be very time-consuming and difficult to try to do this kind of analysis without a computer. The more complex the analysis you undertake, the more difficult it may be to draw conclusions about which you are confident, since the cell size – in other words, the number of responses in each box of your table – may be too small.

Appendix 3
Resources and further reading

ARVAC (2001) *Community Research: Getting Started.* A resource pack for community groups. London: Association for Research in the Voluntary and Community Sector.

Aimed at community groups, this resource pack provides an overview of the research process and guidance on how to plan and design a community research project. It also includes helpful general information on using secondary data and an extensive guide to relevant websites.

Balaswamy, S. and Dabelko, H.I. (2002) 'Using a stakeholder participatory model in a community-wide service needs assessment of elderly residents: a case study', *Journal of Community Practice*, 10(1): 55–70.

American journal article setting out the case for a collaborative approach to community-wide needs assessment as a means of facilitating greater ownership and utilization of controversial findings.

Barnardo's (2000) *What Works? Making Connections: Linking Research and Practice.* Barkingside: Barnardo's.

A report exploring the connections between research and practice in social care. It provides a summary of the factors that help and hinder the application of research to practice.

Bell, J. (2005) *Doing Your Research Project* (4th edn). Maidenhead: Open University Press.

This guide, aimed at all beginning researchers whether students, professionals or practitioners, covers the entire social research process including a chapter on interpreting and presenting evidence.

Blaxter, L., Hughes, C. and Tight, M. (2001) *How to Research* (2nd edn). Buckingham: Open University Press.

This is an excellent reference tool for anybody undertaking community profiles. It
provides practical advice on choosing the most appropriate method, includes
up-to-date material and touches on areas often neglected in other research books,
such as action research techniques and time management. The book looks at the
'writing up' process in some detail, covering grammar, referencing and spelling.

Burgess, T.F. (2001) *Guide to the Design of Questionnaires*, www.leeds.ac.uk/iss/
documentation/top/top2/, accessed 6 December 2006.

This is a clear and easy-to-use tool for those with internet access.

Burns, D. and Taylor, M. (2000) *Auditing Community Involvement: An Assessment
Handbook*. Bristol: The Policy Press.

Provides resources to help map and audit community participation.

Burns, D., Heywood, F., Taylor, M., Wilde, P. and Wilson, M. (2004) *Making Community Participation Meaningful. A Handbook for Development and Assessment*.
Bristol: The Policy Press.

The aim of this publication was to produce a tool which could properly hold
institutions to account for the delivery of meaningful community participation as
a means of encouraging genuine community participation and partnership
working.

Burton, P. (1993) *Community Profiling: A Guide to Identifying Local Needs*. Bristol:
University of Bristol, School for Advanced Urban Studies.

An early, but still useful, guide to the community profiling process.

Carley, M. (2004) *Implementing Community Planning – Building for the Future of Local
Governance*. Edinburgh: Communities Scotland.

Reports on the findings of a study looking at the implementation of community
planning in three cities in Scotland. The purpose of the report was to learn about
the relationship of community planning to participation and service management
and partnership.

Cavanagh, S. (1998) *Making Safer Places. A Resource Book for Neighbourhood Safety
Audits*. London: Women's Design Services.

Intended for use by youth and community workers and volunteers, independent
groups, teachers and individuals who wish to take action to improve the quality

and safety of their urban neighbourhoods. The author takes people through the process of undertaking a community safety audit and provides useful resources to assist with the process.

Christakopoulou, S., Dawson, J. and Gari, A. (2001) 'The community well-being questionnaire: theoretical context and initial assessment of its reliability and validity', *Social Indicators Research*, 56: 321–51.

Argues for a multidimensional approach to measurement of community well-being. Presents the results of a questionnaire used in a pilot area to assess community well-being.

Clark, A. (1996) *Assessing Community Care Needs in a Rural Area: A Report of a Study Carried Out for the North and West Sutherland Community Care Forum*. Lairg: Highland Community Care Forum/Age Concern Scotland/Rural Forum Scotland.

This project arose out of a view among service users and carers, the voluntary and community sector and statutory agencies responsible for community care that a distinctively local approach to assessing needs and developing appropriate solutions was required.

Cockerill, R., Myers, T. and Allman, D. (2000) 'Planning for community-based evaluation', *American Journal of Evaluation*, 21(3): 351–7, http://aje.sagepub.com/cgi/reprint/21/3/351.pdf, accessed 28 March 2007.

In this article the authors present a planning guide that can be used to improve community-based research and evaluation. The guide consists of a set of questions that may be discussed with all stakeholders, covering issues relating to the nature and purpose of a community-based evaluation project, research methods and approaches, participation and decision making, conflict and conflict resolution, and dissemination and use of results.

Department of the Environment, Transport and the Regions (1995) *Involving Communities in Urban and Rural Regeneration. A Guide for Practitioners*. London: DETR.

A manual providing advice to those responsible for regeneration activity at the local level on how to set about involving the community. A bit dated now but still useful. Addresses principles of community involvement, community involvement at each stage of the regeneration process and techniques for involving the community.

Dewar, B., Jones, C. and O'May, F. (2004) *Involving Older People: Lessons for Community Planning*. Edinburgh: Scottish Executive Social Research.

This report examines the level and nature of involving older people in the planning, delivering and monitoring of public services in Scotland. It suggests ways in which that involvement could be improved. The study found a range of mechanisms currently in place offering opportunities for older people to influence some aspects of public services.

Engage East Midlands (2001) *Community Participation: A Self-assessment Toolkit for Partnerships*. Nottingham: Engage East Midlands.

This toolkit was created to give practical assistance to groups wanting to increase the quality and extent of community participation in partnerships they may be involved in. By working through exercises in the toolkit, groups can design partnership strategies and methods to encourage and enable higher levels of community participation.

Epstein, M.H., Quinn, K., Cumblad, C. and Holderness, D. (1996) 'Needs assessment of community-based services for children and youth with emotional or behavioural disorders and their families: Part 1. A conceptual model', *Journal of Mental Health Administration*, 23(4): 418–31.

Presents an overview of a needs assessment model in relation to community-based services for children and young people with emotional or behavioural disorders. The model stresses the need for inter-agency collaboration.

Fallon, G. and Brown, R.B. (2002) 'Focusing on focus groups: lessons from a research project involving a Bangladeshi community', *Qualitative Research*, 2(2): 195–208.

Examines the main issues and challenges associated with the use of the focus group method in a research study involving small business and entrepreneurship.

Fuller, R. and Petch, A. (1995) *Practitioner Research. The Reflexive Social Worker*. Buckingham: Open University Press.

Aimed at practitioners in the social care professions, this book includes chapters on designing a study, methods of collecting and analysing data, and dissemination. It also gives examples of successful research projects undertaken by practitioners.

Green, R. (2000) 'Applying a community needs profiling approach to tackling service user poverty', *British Journal of Social Work*, 30: 287–303.

This article proposes a community profiling approach for use by social workers to enable them to become more aware of the needs of service users and their communities.

Hoggett, P. (ed.) (1997) *Contested Communities: Experiences, Struggles, Policies*. Bristol: The Policy Press.

This book has sections on community and social diversity, local government and community, and community participation and empowerment. Using case studies it examines the ways in which communities define themselves and are defined by outsiders, and developing partnerships with different agencies.

intute, University of Essex (2006) www.vts.intute.ac.uk/tutorial/social-research-methods, accessed 7 November 2006.

Provides a very useful, free guide to using the internet for social research.

Johnson, V. and Webster, J. (2000) *Reaching the Parts . . . Community Mapping: Working Together to Tackle Social Exclusion and Food Poverty*. London: Sustain; The Alliance for Better Food and Farming.

Community mapping project that used participatory appraisal to enable local people to analyse issues in their community and develop solutions to the problems they face. The focus was food and poverty.

Jones, J. and Jones, L. (2002) 'Research and citizen participation', *Journal of Community Work and Development*, 1(3): 50–66.

This article offers a critical view of the increasing amount of community-based research undertaken by public services. In particular it examines four approaches to gathering people's views in terms of how far they increase opportunities for participation.

Kane, E. (2001) *Doing Your Own Research: In the Field and on the Net*. London: Marion Boyars.

This research guide was written to enable non-specialists to do professional and effective research using current technology. It explains all stages of a research project, from developing the basic idea to collecting the information and producing the final paper. Of special interest are chapters on how to use the internet, access databases and improve your communication skills.

Lewis, A. and Lindsay, G. (eds) (2000) *Researching Children's Perspectives*. Buckingham: Open University Press.

This book addresses the issues and practicalities involved in obtaining the views of children. In the first part key theoretical and conceptual issues are discussed; in the second part methods for obtaining children's views are presented, together with their application in specific contexts.

McNeill, P. (1990) *Research Methods*. London: Routledge.

Written for non-specialists, this book discusses key issues of relevance to social research and provides a practical guide to a range of different social research methods.

Murray, S.A. and Graham, L.J.C. (1995) 'Practice-based health needs assessment: use of four methods in a small neighbourhood', *British Medical Journal*, 310: 1443–8.

Compares and contrasts four different methods used to analyse the health needs of a neighbourhood and draws conclusions on the relative contribution of each.

New Economics Foundation (2006) www.neweconomics.org/gen/newways_ socialaudit.aspx/ and www.proveandimprove.org/new/, accessed 31 October 2006.

This is an offshoot of the New Economics Foundation. The website provides interactive tools for social enterprises that are intended to help them measure their impacts and demonstrate the quality of what they do and how they operate.

Nutley, S., Percy-Smith, J. and Solesbury, W. (2003) *Models of Research Impact: A Cross-sector Review of Literature and Practice*. London: Learning and Skills Research Centre.

This publication reports on a project for the Learning and Skills Research Centre that reviewed the literature on research impact and assessed practice in case study organizations. It provides a useful assessment of a number of different strategies for increasing the impact of research.

Open University Library (2001) *Skills in Accessing, Finding and Reviewing Information (SAFARI)*, www.open.ac.uk/safari, accessed 28 March 2007.

This web-based tool is an extremely useful introduction to accessing and using a wide range of different kinds of information.

Packham, C. (1998) 'Community auditing as community development', *Community Development Journal*, 3(3): 249–59.

This article argues that some research methods are inappropriate in a community development context. The author makes the case for a community auditing approach on the grounds that it is more empowering while at the same time producing quantitative and qualitative outcomes.

Patton, M.Q. (1990) *Qualitative Evaluation Methods*. London and Beverly Hills, CA: Sage Publications.

This readable book gives a good account of qualitative data collection, providing useful guidelines for conducting interviews and group work observations. It also contains a useful long bibliography, samples of interview guides, examples of open-ended interviews, and suggested code books for computerized interviews.

Perks, R. and Thompson, A. (1987) *The Oral History Reader*. London: Routledge.

An excellent guide to the topic of oral testimonies, giving a variety of approaches.

Philip, K. (2001) 'Young people's health needs in a rural area: lessons from a participatory rapid appraisal study', *Youth and Policy*, 71: 5–24.

This article reports on a research project that set out to elicit the views on health of young people in a rural area. A participatory rapid appraisal approach was adopted and the paper considers the advantages and disadvantages of using this approach.

Regeneris Consulting (2002) *Community Profiling Guidance Notes*, North West Museums Service (NWMS), available at www.inspiringlearningforall.org/ uploads/Community%20Profiling%20Guidan.pdf.

This report was commissioned to enable the NWMS to work more strategically in directly targeting the needs of particular communities of interest. It provides a quantitative profile of various communities of interest, both across the north-west region as a whole and in particular local areas.

Reid, P.T. (2001) 'Negotiating partnerships in research on poverty with community-based agencies', *Journal of Social Issues*, 57(2): 337–54.

Argues for the participation of people within communities being researched (in this case poor women). Strategies for securing cooperation are discussed and described.

Renewal.net has produced an online 'How to do it' document giving a practical introduction on how to carry out a community audit. It looks at a number of key stages, including getting started on planning the audit, carrying it out, results and recommendations, reporting, and acting on the results. Like community profiling, it emphasizes the need to involve the community at every stage. It introduces some of the techniques used and gives details about other resources. It also helps you to decide whether to bring in outside help on some or all of the work, discusses writing a brief for the work and how to assess any bids to undertake it. The manual can be downloaded at www.renewal.net/ Documents/RNET/Toolkit/Howcarryout.doc.

Rural Community Network has resource fact sheets for community development on its website: www.ruralcommunitynetwork.org (in the online publications page). There is a fact sheet about community audits at http://pub. ruralcommunitynetwork.org/files/pdf/Community%20Audits.pdf.

Rural Development Council (2002) *Learning Communities Resource Pack*. This workbook is designed for community facilitators who are working with communities to identify local needs. It also focuses on producing action plans for addressing those needs. Available from Rural Development Council, 17 Loy Street, Cookstown, Northern Ireland BT80 8PZ, tel. (028) 8676 6980, www.rdc.org.uk, accessed March 2007.

SCARF (2006) (www.scdc.org.uk.) The Scottish Community Action Research Fund (SCARF) gives community groups support to improve their skills and confidence to carry out their own research. The fund helps them to plan a project, collect information and understand it, use the information and learn from the experience.

Schonlau, M., Fricker, R.D. Jr and Elliott, M.N. (2002) *Conducting Research Surveys via E-mail and the Web*. Santa Monica, CA: RAND.

This book is full of information and background and is an essential read before considering any online survey. A hard copy can be purchased or it can be downloaded free at www.rand.org/pubs/monograph_reports/MR1480/.

Scott, J. (2002) *Assessing the Housing Needs and Demands of BME Communities in West Dunbartonshire*. A report to Communities Scotland. Edinburgh: Communities Scotland.

Study involving a quantitative analysis of the BME population in West Dunbartonshire; fieldwork to gain an understanding of how services are delivered and the housing experiences of BME households.

Scottish Executive (2004) *The Local Government Act in Scotland, 2003. Community Planning Advice Notes*. Edinburgh: Scottish Executive.

Useful publication describing the relationship of community plans to national priorities and providing advice on various aspects of the community planning process. Each section ends with relevant web links and further reading.

Sharp, C. (n.d.) *Finsbury Park Community Profile*. A research report for the Finsbury Park Community Regeneration Initiative. London: University of North London.

Research to identify the assets or 'social capital' of the area as a contribution to the development of a regeneration strategy.

Skinner, S. (1998) *Building Community Strengths*. London: Community Development Foundation.

This book is aimed at community workers in different settings. It purpose is to increase understanding of the nature of collective capacity building and its potential for communities. Five sections discuss: 'What is capacity building?'; 'Developing people'; 'Developing organizations'; 'Developing community infrastructure'; and 'Developing plans and strategies'.

Smith, G. (2002) 'Community research: a practitioner's perspective on methods and values', *Journal of Community Work and Development*, 1(3), http://homepages.uel.ac.uk/G.Smith/communityresearch.pdf.

This article examines some of the issues that arise when attempting community-based research. It explores the tension between the need for professional standards and the possibilities of empowerment through do-it-yourself research. It also looks at the notion of research on a shoestring and some free resource points are mentioned. It explores assumptions about appropriate quantitative and qualitative methods.

Smith, M.K. (2001) 'Community', in *The Encyclopaedia of Informal Education*, www.infed.org/community/community.htm, last updated 28 January 2005.

This article examines the concept of community, exploring the development of theory and ways in which the word is used by sociologists and social theorists. It examines the main concepts needed to make sense of the idea in practice, that is boundary, norms and habits, and social capital.

Tarling, R. (2006) *Managing Social Research: A Practical Guide*. London: Routledge.

This book is an introduction to managing social research projects. Although it is predominantly aimed at researchers working in organizations, it contains much that is useful for those managing community-based research projects.

Taylor, M. (2003) *Public Policy in the Community*. Basingstoke: Palgrave.

This book explores the way that community and other related ideas have been used in policy since the 1960s.

Tennant, R. and Long, G. (1998) *Community Profile Resource Pack*. Glasgow: Glasgow Caledonian University.

This is an information pack for local groups who wish to develop a community profile to present evidence about the needs and resources in their area. It provides guidance on planning the community profile, setting aims and objectives, identifying relevant issues and analysing the data. It also provides guidance on publicity, presenting information in an effective way and getting your message across.

University of Leicester (2004) *Exploring Online Research Methods in a Virtual Training Environment*, available at www.geog.le.ac.uk/orm/site/home_alt.htm, accessed 6 December 2006.

This is an ESRC-funded project that aims to 'enhance understanding of online research methods through the production and evaluation of a self-supporting online training package targeted at the social science community'.

Wates, N. (1996) *Action Planning. How to Use Planning Weekends and Urban Design Action Teams to Improve your Environment.* London: Prince of Wales's Institute of Architecture.

This handbook describes what is involved in running an 'action planning' event aimed at improving a local area. It incorporates useful advice based on previous experiences and tools, checklists and ideas that can be adapted for local use.

Wates, N. (2000) *The Community Planning Handbook.* London: Earthscan.

This is a practical guide to community planning, giving a menu of tools available for community planning from design workshops to electronic maps. Tips, checklists and sample documents are provided to help you get started quickly. It can be downloaded from www.communityplanning.net or www.nickwates.co.uk/.

Wilcox, D. (1994) *The Guide to Effective Participation*, Brighton: Delta Press.

This guide is aimed at those wanting to encourage community involvement. It addresses a wide range of issues including how to run effective public meetings, when it is best to use surveys or to get residents involved in building a model of the future, and the differences between consultation, participation, partnership and empowerment.

Software for data analysis

As we said in Chapter 8, there are many computer software packages available for quantitative and qualitative data analysis; this is a very small selection of the more commonly used ones. Many of these packages are available to be downloaded as trial versions from the websites listed.

Qualitative analysis software

ATLAS.ti   See: www.atlasti.com/

Version 5 is a user-friendly and flexible package that allows coding and annotation of text, images, and many formats of audio and video, and html pages. It has a network mapping feature for visual display as well as good search features. Although there is no Mac version, ATLAS.ti will run on Macs using virtual PC software.

The Ethnograph See: www.qualisresearch.com/

This was one of the first qualitative analysis programs. It allows direct transfer of text from any word-processor format to the program. It has good code and retrieval features.

QSR NVivo See: www.qsrinternational.com/products/productoverview/NVivo_7.htm

Version 7 allows you to edit documents as you code (most programs do not) and also font colours (via Rich Text Format file format). Again, there is only a Windows version and not one for Macs. It allows linking to external documents for audio and video and, unusually, has movable screen windows.

Survey and statistical software

SPSS See: www.spss.com/

SPSS has a number of modules. The data entry module and base modules would be sufficient to enter and store data and then analyse it. However, additional modules are required for quality graphical and tabular output. SPSS is not as easy to use as the dedicated community profiling software, and can often be user-unfriendly to those inexperienced in using such packages. However, having learned how to use it, SPSS is extremely powerful and can undertake as much statistical analysis as one could ever require from survey data (and, for community profiling, a lot more).

SPSS has recently bought another leading survey creation and data collection software-producing company, Quantime. The merger of the two companies' products has produced another easy-to-use and very powerful market research package. For further details see www.spss.com/vertical_markets/survmkt_research/.

Snap See: www.snapsurveys.com/

Snap supports all survey techniques including web, email, paper and phone surveys. The data can be entered, stored and analysed, and tables generated. Frequencies and cross-tabulations can easily be produced. It claims MS Access or SQL database connectivity and seamless integration with SPSS and MS Office (Word, Excel, PowerPoint, Access).

Index